To Melissa,
You are His Souls' ...!
May He be ...
cry~ May

Love for you
Mom
Acts 20:24

MW00462315

SOUL CRY

PAM JENKINS

The cry of the soul to go farther than it can see.

First printing

Joy Publications has allowed this work to remain exactly as the author intended, verbatim, without editorial input.

"Scripture taken from the New American Standard Bible Copyright 1960, 1962, 1963, 1968, 1971, 1972, 1973, 1975, 1977, 1995 by the Lockman Foundation. Used by permission." (www.lockman.org) Scripture quotations identified KJV are from the King James Version.

ISBN: 978-1-5323-3076-6

Published by Joy Publications Inc.
Atlanta, GA,

To contact the author or for permission to copy or use please visit; www.jabbokministries.com for direct contact information.

Printed in the United States of America

I bow before You, looking to Your holy temple, and praise Your name, for Your unfailing love and Your truth…

On the day I needed You, I called, and You responded and infused my soul with strength

———

PSALM 138:2 & 3, THE VOICE

INTRODUCTION

I've searched deeply and painstakingly for the words that would describe for you this book you hold in your hand. There is a simplicity of any ability this author might have. I am not a writer, I am a servant…a bondservant. I am but a hand willing to put upon paper, the thoughts and understandings God has given to me, His laborer.

I share with you, what He has shared with me. Each page of this book, every paragraph, every word, has been penned through prayer. The journey ahead has been forged from the chamber of my soul as God has spoken. He has been writing it for 55 years. May these simple words bring greatness to the glory of God and may they speak to your soul as God has spoke to mine.

When all is said and done, when you have read every last word of these pages, I pray you will surmise the same conclusion I have for living:

There is but one cry Heaven aches, groans and even yearns for…a Soul Cry.

CONTENTS

I can't remember exactly the first time your soul whispered to mine but I know you woke it, and it has never slept since.

———

JM STORM

CHAPTER ONE

AWAKE MY SOUL

The sound was irrefutable. No question as to what it was or from where it came. It pierced through the atmosphere of the unseen with such force, that all who heard it knew history would be forever changed. Eternity had inscribed a name upon the pages of time, leaving the footprints of God Himself to bear witness throughout the ages.

We were penetrated to the very soul of our being as time seemed to stand still, encircling us in the wonder of the indescribable. We were captives of what God had done; vessels of hope for what was yet to be.

The sound itself was not new to the world stage, yet it had never been heard before. Not until this moment of which I now write. We've all heard it before; we have all been living megaphones through which it has poured forth.

And we've been such from our beginning.

There are no words for such splendor sealed up in a single moment of existence for our viewing. Somehow, in some way, we knew we had been swept into a remarkable encounter. Heaven had drenched our hearts with waters of such grace and beauty, that all sorrow of life rolled away upon the distant shores of the forgotten.

We would never recover from such a colossal feat poured out upon us from the hand of the Almighty.

The day Heaven bends down to crown your life and His world with such a gift, is an eternal wonder. And we beheld His beauty there, living witnesses of God's unfailing faithfulness. How grateful we were to be invited into such a place of desperation for Him; A time when we were privileged to give God our everything. We knew we had been chosen for such a time as this. Our hearts were united for God to have His will and His way, whatever the outcome.

We had anticipated, even longed for, this day knowing that this was *the Lord's doing and it was marvelous in our eyes* (Psalm 118:23). Although we had only waited for nine months, it was a lifetime of anticipation rallying together for the glory of the Creator. The labor was intense. The room congregated with the necessary staff, enlarging the reality at hand. Our little Stella was making her grand entrance into our lives and into God's world.

Her birth was no ordinary occurrence, not because she was my granddaughter, but because she was given a death sentence in the womb. Early on, in my daughter's pregnancy, they discovered a problem with her undeveloped brain. Scan after scan, consultation after consultation, all resulted in the same advice from the doctors; terminate the pregnancy. Medical advice from a human perspective can sometimes be void of love and absent of faith, just when the soul needs it the most.

Stella's diagnosis was grim and heartbreaking. The probability of her surviving any length of time was bleak and if she did, her life would be challenging and without a doubt…shortened. According to man, there was little or no hope.

We weren't seeking a miracle in this moment I write of, we believed Stella was the miracle. There are those life moments where our faith must collide with our overwhelming need, facing it down, fully trusting in God and what we know to be true about Him. This was that time.

My daughter Stephanie along with her husband Jonathan, were so brave in the face of such challenge. Having been advised by the doctors to terminate the pregnancy, that word was never given a place of occupancy in their hearts and minds. Jonathan declared months earlier, *"Whatever God has for us is good and perfect."*

In this truth, we have nothing to fear.

How that bears repeating: Whatever God has for us is good and perfect. Absolutely nothing, not even death itself or uncertainty of the future, can alter who God is to us and who we are to Him.

Fear has no place in the realm of truth. It loses all power upon this battleground of hope.

Truth will disarm every anxious thought and take it captive to accomplish its will. It has the yoke of ability to harness unsettled emotions, drawing the heart back within the confines of hope and stability of settled assurance. We had warred according to this understanding and the peace of God held us there.

When God invades our realities, His love overpowers all fear. *There is no fear in love; perfect love casts out all fear* (1 John 4:18). His love may not always be understood or easily identified, but it is always perfect. Fear must retreat and remain powerless in the presence of the love of God.

It is profoundly life-changing when the soul comes to experience the grip of God's love in the face of unbearable sorrow. Fear is but a shadow of powerless intrusion that must be given permission to stay. In the love of God, and in the name of Jesus, we courageously forbade fear to take up residency in our midst.

Hours passed. Finally, after checking my daughter's labor progression, it was announced that the baby would be coming soon. I wanted to shout to the Heavens, *"STELLA IS ON HER WAY TO US!"* Of course, to avoid severe embarrassment for my precious first born, as well as for my "son-n-love", I somehow restrained myself.

Even in this great resolve of self-control, my heart was pounding with such joy and trust in the gift God was bringing into His world and into our lives. The unknown was about to become known and we praised God on the front side of it. That announcement was all it took.

They seemed to converge from nowhere. The medical staff amassed in the labor and delivery room capable and fearless. The doctor had made herself ready and the necessary equipment was brought in and set up. The special team of skilled hands prepared to do what they were highly trained to do. It was a common occurrence for them…just a "walk in the park" it seemed. Their hands were steady and sure.

In the heartbeat of this moment, I wondered if they had any idea what holy grandeur they were a part of that day. Ordinary events can bring with them eternal workings that have been wrought over time, never revealing its presence. How often and unknowingly, our lives brush against eternity; converging ordinary life events with the soul work of God.

Our hearts were anchored deeply in not only the love of God, but in His perfect will.

Through the hours of painful labor and at times agonizing waiting, we heard the heartbeat of baby Stella resounding through the monitor. It was Heaven's megaphone of hope taking command of every other outside noise and internal struggle that tried to emerge within. The echo of her existence resonated in our room.

We knew that a life was there, and it was coming.

Transitioning from the womb to the world was the immediate journey ahead of her. Until that passage of change is made, life is held in the balance of uncertainty and anticipation; veiling from our view the beautiful soul yet to be born. The road upon which we had traversed to arrive at this time and place had been laid one prayer at a time; stone upon stone of relentless intercession.

Countless prayers had been offered up on her behalf with fervency and fasting. We treasured and coveted every one of them. We believed God was in our midst. He would be her escort into this world.

I'm so grateful that babies have no knowledge of the world or their condition at birth. Stella was unaware of the diagnosis pronounced over her unborn life. She was not bound to a future or existence established for her by the word or diagnosis of man. Of these things, she was not a captive. They would not define her. Her future and very existence hinged on none of these things because she was not the work of man.

She was the masterpiece of the Creator.

Mortal words would prove powerless in the face of her coming. No human force or persuasion can define a soul or determine the value or length of a life. These are the untouchables, defined by Heaven for us. Held in the grip of Sovereignty. Baby Stella, as every baby is, was safeguarded in this protected place.

There's that moment of sacred silence as the doctor turns and positions the baby to assist it on this process we call birth. We waited with baited breath, hearts rapidly beating, longing to see, to know, to touch and to hold this precious wonder. It was as if Stella could hear the anthem of Judges 5:21 declaring, *"Oh my soul, march on with strength."*

Sometimes, the soul needs an anthem to steer it on its way.

How would Stella make her grand entrance?

Would it be with thunderous applause or shouts of joy and acclamation?

First her head appeared, of which we could see was covered with this dark thick hair. Slowly, and with great care, the doctor drew her forth for all to see. Piercing through the holy hush of silence, commanding the delivery room, came the first sound of the soul, the first language of all life.

A cry.

A soul's cry.

A cry so strong and enveloping, that we understood all life is a miracle. There are no accidents, no unwanted, none who are outcasts or mistakes. It wasn't a cry to be heard, it was a cry to be felt and known. A cry from the soul that announces, "I LIVE… I LIVE!" Mortal words are, at best, intrusive in the time of such miraculous discoveries.

Stella's soul had a voice!

We knew that angels had assembled to celebrate the soul crying out for life. This is the great wonder to breathe in. Let this understanding find a lodging place within: The soul communicates long before the mouth learns to speak. Heaven needs no words, no language to translate the existence of or the need of human life.

The soul has a language all its own.

The soul's cry is a birthright given to every living being. It cannot be penned, printed or forged within the framework of human effort. How does one write or spell it out? Paper and ink cannot contain or translate it for us. It collides with the Creator on a level that cannot be articulated. The cry of the newborn is but an exhale of the breath of the Almighty. That first breath of life breathed into the soul comes from Him, and the resounding praise that it echoes is the language that every soul knows. A cry.

Even though it's been four years since Stella was born, the encounter is still fresh and powerfully moving to all of us. She's perfect, all praise to God! He healed her, to the astonishment of the medical staff. But not to us. Her birth day is a memorial of faith for our family.

The soul of Stella cried out that day and Heaven responded. God knelt down upon the shallows of the earth, and breathed life into her tiny lungs, validating her soul's existence and branding her as *"belonging to Him."*

Louie Giglio said, *"Worship is simply giving God back His breath."* God breathes in and the soul cries out in testimony to this union. Like any other baby, baby Stella had no need for anyone to teach her how to cry out. She learned it from Him, her Mighty Creator. He wrote this ability upon the tablet of the heart. This is the first language the soul speaks and the first communication between God and His child.

A newborn's cry is the untainted form of dialog in the universe. This first cry is unadulterated, unschooled, not taught by human flesh or held by earthly force. It is wholly transparent, uninhibited, and without pretense. It is not deceptive, calculating, manipulative or self-seeking, and it is altogether a captivating mystery to behold.

Despite the absence of words, it speaks volumes to those privileged to encounter it. It is simply the soul's way of communicating when the mouth can't speak on its behalf.

What a mysterious entity the human soul is. It has known the breath of God and dialogued with Him who is Holy. This beautiful cry of the soul is music to Heaven and a symphony in the ears of the earth, beginning with all of us who were in the room. It's profoundly timeless and transcendent, able to reach the deepest place of the heart. It is the purest form of communion, praise, and worship that we can hear this side of Heaven.

When Stella was crying out in the labor and delivery room, to whom was she crying? She didn't know anyone in the room. Her eyes had not yet seen anything or anyone except the brightness of the light filling the room. She had only known the darkness of the womb.

To whom did she cry to?

Why did she cry?

Who taught her to do so?

I believe God gives a glimpse of the answer in His Word. Although, the following passage is not one of poetic beauty at first reading, and the details a bit gory, I want you to see the heart and rule of God. These words are recorded for us in the Old Testament book of Ezekiel 16:4-6:

As for your birth, on the day you were born your navel cord was not cut, nor were you washed with water for cleansing; you were not rubbed with salt or even wrapped in cloths.

No eye looked with pity on you to do any of these things for you, to have compassion on you. Rather, you were thrown out into the open field, for you were abhorred on the day you were born.

When I passed by you and saw you squirming in your blood, I said to you while you were in your blood, "Live!" Yes, I said to you while you were in your blood, "Live!".

It does not matter if every other person has dismissed a birth as nothing, or wrote it off as meaningless and hopeless, God has the final word. He is the One your soul responds to. You and I are His soul work. Your soul knew Him first and your soul will know Him last. He established Himself as your Alpha and Omega, your beginning and your end while you were still in your mother's womb.

You began with Him.

It's a working shrouded in supremacy, cloaked in holy mystery. Understand this glorious truth: On the day of your birth, He looked at you and cried, *"LIVE! LIVE!"* Just as He did baby Stella that day. He is your life giver and He is your life sustainer. Your faithful God.

There was a day that you too let out your first cry. There was a day when you cried out to your God. Your soul has this imprint of remembrance upon it and there it has remained all the days of your life.

Human language fails to describe the inspiring marvel of a baby's cry. Words aren't necessary because they are inadequate. They are comforting and reassuring for those in the birthing room and for the medical staff. They all anticipate that first cry usually with no thought of the intimacy that has been taking place between Creator God and His child. Our eyes are focused on the physical, the immediate in front of us; that which is seen.

Hear the words of King David preserved for us in Psalm 139:14. *"I will give thanks to You, for I am fearfully and wonderfully made; Wonderful are Your works, and my soul knows it very well."*

I believe a newborn's first cry signifies something even greater than, *"I live,"* it declares; *"I live because of Him!"*

Adoration without words.

Wordless worship and praise.

The first cry of the soul is to live, and in the living, acknowledge its Creator. They have been intimately acquainted for months, shut off from the outside world and influences. Only God, instilling in the soul of His child, His very self and knowledge of His existence.

This is the first learning of the soul: ***My life is found in Him.***

From the depths of the soul, we communicate with God. This is what He has taught us before we were even born, before our first breath. He wanted us to know this first, before the philosophies and doctrines of the world got a hold of us. God understands the language of a cry; the language of the soul.

It comes from the deepest part of our being. He wrote it and He taught it to us…to you. This was His gift to you, a way for you to talk with Him when there are no words to be found.

It is, in its simplest form, unfailing dialogue.

This is what God knows about all life. When words fail, when our circumstances are too hard, and life is unbearable, our soul can cry out. There are groaning's in this life that are so painful, so unreachable and unthinkable, that there are simply no words to convey what the heart longs to say (Romans 8:26). And from this most sacred and untouchable place, God hears you and speaks to you.

Listen to the words of the Psalmist in 57:2, *"I will cry to God Most High, to God who accomplishes all things for me,"* and again, in Psalm 77:1, *"My voice rises to God, and I will cry aloud; My voice rises to God, and He will hear me."*

It gives for us fresh insight and renowned beauty as we consider Psalm 139:4 which says, *"Even before there is a word on my tongue, Behold, Oh LORD, Thou dost know it all."*

God knows the thoughts and the cries of the soul. God did not make your words distinctive, but He did make your cry distinctive. Your cry is different from all others.

When my girls were babies, I would put them in the nursery at church, so I could attend the service. If I was ever in earshot of the baby area, it would not matter how many babies were crying, I knew mine above all others. All mothers can attest to this truth. Their cry was unquestionably unique to them.

My grandbabies are no different. I have been blessed with seven such miracles, at the writing of this book. Each grandchild's cry has been altogether different and set apart from the others. A parent, especially a mother, will recognize her child's cry above all the others.

Why?

Because each soul's cry is a mastery all its own, bestowed upon them by the Creator. It cannot be mimicked or disguised. It is unmistakable in its identity.

Just as a mother, or Grammy, can identify her child's (or grand-child's) cry, so God recognizes and knows the cry of His child. On the day of your birth, your first cry ascended to the throne of God: A day when your soul exclaimed to the world, *"I live, I live"* *and "I live because of Him."*

Although you have no remembrance of this, Heaven does. God does. All who were present do.

It was your soul's first statement of faith; A faith not taught by human tongue, your birth mother, any attending medical help, or family. Whoever was there or wasn't there, heaven and earth both bore witness of your soul's first cry. The sound of your soul declaring your arrival and validating the work of God.

A cry is the most powerful and captivating of sounds. Anywhere we are, whether it be in a crowd, outside in the yard or in the house, in a doctor's office, on an airplane or anywhere else we may find ourselves, a cry has the power to stop us in our tracks. It draws us in and causes us to take notice. It sounds the alarm that something is wrong or that something is right. It engages our attention, even from a perfect stranger.

The cry is universal yet, no two cries are the same. We all speak this language. It knows no geographic boundaries, ethnic ties, religious beliefs, or necessary dialects. It stands alone. It speaks on many levels apart from words, without sentence or speech. It can cry out in praise or raise a cry in pain and never need an interpreter.

It was your first act of living. The day your soul learned to cry out. No one can take the glory for this ability but your Creator, God. He is your soul's beginning point and there at this sacred place of sovereignty, He speaks your language and He communes with your soul.

Your soul cry…**It is your unfailing dialogue with Heaven.**

Our souls met long before our eyes did

—

A . P .

CHAPTER TWO

A WORK OF SOUL

What treasures and wounds a little girl will tuck away in her memory. Things that haunt her, rob her and give to her, protect her and hurt her. Threads of events weaving a garment of identity for her to wear for all of her days. Aristotle said, *"The memory is the scribe of the soul."* We may never know the impact of a single moment of life until we have viewed it from the other side, through the lens of our remembrance.

The soul becomes a reservoir of many things, good and bad, drawing up the waters of bitterness along with the sweet. It's the uniqueness of God's design. When a soul is born it has this ability to store up events, faces, emotion, pain, joy and more. This little soul grows up one day. But even though adulthood has been attained, deep in the well of remembrance, the soul continues to draw from the waters of yesterday, leaving it thirsty and unfulfilled.

The soul has a voice and it speaks to us. It calls to us. The world calls it, our "inner self", or our "inner child." It has the unique ability to speak out of what has passed and into what will be. It's been said that if we quiet the mind, the soul will speak. Like a voice from yesterday, recalling the former things into the present.

It is a force of great strength having the power to move, disturb, settle, thwart, and even shut down or raise up. Ferdinand Fouch said it best, "*The most powerful weapon on earth is the human soul on fire.*" A soul has the distinct ability to strike a match within, burning a path it will trod all the days of its life.

How inimitable the human soul.

Growing up, I agonized over the way I looked. I disliked everything about that little girl. My face, my size, my feet, my teeth, my nose. You name it, there was nothing good about me in my own eyes. Through the bullhorn of my skewed view, I spoke death into my own life. Not because I was told these things. Quite the opposite.

My mother reinforced that I was special and that I was beautiful. I was highly loved and encouraged by my mother and grandparents. But that made no difference in my vision of dislike. I rehearsed my own negativity until the lie I was feeding my soul became my reality. My soul believed what my mind was teaching. The mirror I held up told me a different story.

Hear the words of the Apostle Paul, in 1Corinthians 13:11-12:

> "*When I was a child, I used to speak like a child,*
> *think like a child, reason like a child; when I became a man,*
> *I did away with childish things.*

*For now, we see in a mirror dimly, but then
face to face; now I know in part, but then I will know fully
just as I also have been fully known."*

Our child, (the soul) Paul says, knows how to speak, think and reason. The mirror in his hand is obscure; dimmed by the things of the earth. Mirrors reflect what we put in front of it. If we put a lie in front of the mirror, it will speak it back to us.

Our mirrors have been speaking, but what have they been telling us?

Growing up, I was small for my age, extremely hyper, had reddish hair with freckles adorning my nose. You could have asked any of my teachers and especially my mama, and they would have told you the same; I had no self-control. It was who I was. If I thought it, I said it, and I was wildly active with a very poor sense of confidence.

Because of the low thoughts I had of myself, I turned to my comedic side to make people laugh. Goofy skits and songs were always in the making upon my overly imaginative brain. If I didn't love myself, then I had established that no one else must either. But this is what I put in front of the mirror of my soul. So, in response, I set out to earn their love through entertainment.

It was an external fix for an internal problem.

I can remember hearing the words for the first time as a young woman, *"Before you can love others, you've got to learn to love yourself."* It was a difficult concept for me to lay ahold of, since

I didn't even like myself, let alone love me. How was I to love someone who in my eyes was unlovable?

Doomed from the onset, I had believed this partial truth for many years. Do we really need to love ourselves? Is it wrong… self-centered or selfish?

After I became a Christian, I came to believe that it was wrong to love yourself. It sounded conceited and out of reach for me. There was just something about this thinking that bothered me and alluded my understanding of it. It was a far reach from the words of Jesus in Matthew 16:24 which says: …*If anyone wishes to come after Me, he must deny himself, and take up his cross and follow Me.*

Deny yourself seems to imply the opposite of loving yourself, at least in my feeble thinking. In the naivety of my early faith, and for many years after, I had reconciled hating myself with following Jesus. My soul was lost to the truth. It had to find its way back to the beginning, so it could start again.

When we read the words of King Solomon recorded for us in Proverbs 19:8, our perspective begins to shift. Listen to what he says: *He who gets wisdom loves his own soul; He who keeps understanding will find good.*

It's not just self that we should love (contrary to what the world is teaching). That's not quite the fullness of truth given to us. It's the soul that is to be loved. We must learn to love our soul and to love it as God has loved it. He placed the highest value upon the soul, setting it like a seal upon the love of His heart.

Hear the words of Jesus concerning this truth found in Matthew 16:26: *For what will it profit a man, if he gains the whole world and forfeits his soul? Or what will a man give in exchange for his soul?*

According to the words of Jesus, the soul is the most valued possession of all life. It is an eternal entity and the most important arena of living we can dwell in. *"There was a time when your soul was not, but there will never be a time when your soul will not be"* (Dr. Benny Tate – slight variation). The soul will live on forever, long after the body has expired.

You don't have a soul, you are a soul. What you choose to do with this treasured gift is of the greatest importance. In fact, there is nothing more significant than the soul… your soul…nothing. With this knowledge, comes great responsibility.

What gives the soul its intrinsic value?

What dictates its worth?

When we turn our attention back to the very beginning of time, as we know it, the answer begins to slip into view. But as we will come to find out, it will beckon us to go deeper. Truth is not learned, it must be revealed.

Genesis 2:7 draws the curtain back for our enlightenment and shines the spotlight upon the soul for the first time in Scripture:

Then the LORD God formed man of dust from the ground and breathed into his nostrils the breath of life; and man became a living soul (KJV).

The meaning for the word soul used in this passage refers to our will, emotions, inner self and thinking. It's the "who" of who we are, the very life dwelling within our physical bodies! It's what makes you, you. *"It is the sacred essence of who we are. The guiding force behind our individual lives"* (Mateo Sol).

Scripture records for us that God breathed into man, and he became a living soul. Adam was not a living soul until the breath of God filled his lungs. It was the very breath of God that raised the soul to life. And the journey began. A journey that has been progressing since birth.

Understand and know this prevailing truth of your existence. Laying hold of it, will prove to be a spiritual compass for your life:

THE SOUL'S FIRST NEED FOR LIFE, WAS THE BREATH OF GOD.

The breath of God is necessary for the soul to be raised in newness of life. If we look back to the time before the soul took its first breath, we see how and when God laid this path of need for us. We must see the unborn soul. And we can do that only through the eyes of our Creator.

Psalm 139:5, 13-16 allows us to see through the eyes of God to behold the incredible creation of life as it is taking place. These verses take us into the very womb of conception, unveiling the marvel of God's wondrous work. Let these sacred words find a lodging place within you. Read them slowly and purposefully, giving them the needed time to rest in your heart and mind. These words are the DNA of who you are, and our DNA is unchanging as God has purposed it to be.

> *You have enclosed me behind and before;*
> *and laid Thy hand upon me.*

> *For You did form my inward parts; You did*
> *weave me in my mother's womb.*

> *I will give thanks to You, for I am fearfully*
> *and wonderfully made; wonderful are Your*
> *works, and my **soul** knows it very well.*

> *My frame was not hidden from You when*
> *I was made in secret…*

> *Your eyes have seen mine unformed substance, and in*
> *Your book, they were all written, the days that were ordained*
> *for me, when as yet there was not one of them.*

This tapestry of truth is stitched with such threads of wonder, the Psalmist could barely take it in. You can hear the waves of the miraculous crashing over his very soul, as the greatness of God's might swell before his eyes. Yet he declares, *My soul knows it very well.*

The soul has the propensity to know, even when the ability to explain or understand is absent. Without a shadow of doubt, there is the settled conviction of the work and design of God. It has the capacity to adhere its faith to this constant.

There is a covert place where no human hand can take the credit for what occurs. In this dwelling of the unseen, the soul is a student of the Holy One. There is a tutoring of the soul taking place, a learning not from the lowliness of earthly wisdom given by human hand.

As this infinite truth rises before the eyes of the Psalmist, he resonates this grand profession of faith before his God; *I am your work…and my soul knows it very well.* He speaks from the perspective of the unborn soul; the soul still in the womb of life. He writes of a knowledge that is too miraculous for words, an immensity of power beyond human comprehension.

The whispers of origin fall into the ears, and there, find an inescapable place of permanence: *For You formed my inward parts; You wove me in my mother's womb* (v 13).

This is the very heartbeat of this sacred passage. Through it, we discover that the soul has been given a divine revelation of its making. This school of learning was the first and it will never leave its consciousness. It has been forever branded deeply, for all eternity.

There are some striking word meanings in this passage of scrutiny that are imperative for us to know. Bear with me as I share these with you. Drink them in and see what God has done; what He has taught the soul to remember. Heaven has inscribed it here, so you will know.

You did form my inward parts, he declares. The term, *"inward parts",* refers to the seat of emotion and affection, the mind or interior of self. The word *"formed"*, means to create, possess, purchase or own. When we read the verse back with the word meanings inserted, it tells us this: My inward self, the deepest part of me, you created for your very own, establishing owner-ship, while I was still in the womb.

This intentional usage is a picture of the soul for us. It speaks of the inward being of a person. He is the maker of the human soul. You are His workmanship, brought about in the secret place of the womb of life. In the depth of you, God left His mark of authenticity, the culmination of your unique make up…your undeniable DNA.

Listen to the words of the Prophet Isaiah in Isaiah 64:8: *But now, O LORD, Thou art our father; we are the clay, and Thou our potter; and we all are the work of Thy hand.*

God is the potter and we are His clay. There was a time when your soul responded to God's touch, yielding to His every way, the heartbeat of His will and Word. In the depths of you, you know what it is to surrender unto Him completely.

Looking to the words of the Psalmist once again, we read, *You did weave me in my mother's womb.* The word, *"weave"* gives us a beautiful understanding of the relationship that is taking place. It means to hedge in, cover, overshadow or join together. Before you took your first breath, God established the existence of His presence.

Validation of the soul's beginning does not hinge on whether the soul acknowledges its commencement. It is forever settled in Heaven, having been written by God, sealing up its eternal authority. The soul is not the author of truth, it is the recipient of it. He gave you origin before He gave you life, and before He gave you breath. Nothing beyond that first breath will ever change or alter the permeance of God's seal upon His child.

This is the foundation from which all life finds its footing for the land of the living. Launching out on anything different will end in eternal loss. He is your refuge, your life source, your first soul mate, and your first love.

Your soul has a forever union with God. In the workings of His creative power and design, He wrapped His arms about you, sur-rounding you with Himself on every side. Before the arms of human flesh would ever hold you, you were cradled in Sovereignty. Before your eyes viewed another, you saw Him. His face etched into your memory as He drew near to breathe in the breath of life.

He was your first teacher. The womb is the most vital place of learning because it is here the soul comes to know the eternal things; those things that will never be removed from its memory. Here, the soul learns the very touch of God, His nearness and His presence. He is weaving and creating the life of His child; the soul that He loves and that He Himself designed. God marked you as His very own; writing across the canvas of you, *She belongs to me.*

You may not feel wanted, but God wanted you first. Before you could speak, walk, serve, choose, act or think; He wanted you. He declared over you, *"I want her."* This love and cherished affection upon you is not based on anything you did or would do one day, or even on what you would become. It is based solely on the soul of God.

His work is perfect, lacking nothing. His love was extended to you without the demand of reciprocation. It was given in full measure, pressed down and overflowing, apart from performance and without demands.

Your soul is loved just as it is, and it has been from the very beginning. God's love is unconditional and unending.

He is before you, because He saw your unformed substance. Before the first day of your life existed, when there was not yet one of them. The Creator viewed the length and breadth of your life and at the very end of it, He placed Himself. It is grand and altogether farther than the eye can see.

And herein lies a most extraordinary mystery: God designed and created your soul to go farther than what it can see.

Knowing Him, cannot be accredited to our line of sight. It must come from the lineage of what is unseen, but not unknown. This you will come to understand is the soul's journey, it's stretching to lay hold of this abiding and unchanging truth. And hidden in the crevice of this reach, is the fullness and wonder of the enduring love of God.

There has never been a day of your life when you were not loved by God because He loved you before your first breath was ever taken. He loved you first and cultivated within you, from the onset of conception, intimacy with the Creator. The soul and God began an eternal communion long before the ears were formed, or the tongue fashioned.

Soul to soul, God did His most excellent work, forging a bond that would last for all of eternity. A soul tie never to be broken. It begins before the first breath is taken but resonates with every exhale decanted in the land of the living.

Genesis 1:27 teaches this to us: *God created man in His own image, in the image of God He created him; male and female He created them.*

We are made in His likeness, in the image of Him; giving your soul intrinsic worth. He gave you your soul with the intention of binding Himself to you; soul to soul. His soul to yours for all of time. The seal of the Creator was impressed upon the tablet of your heart.

You are a work of soul…His soul.

Bear with me as we see this thought-provoking truth and maybe one you've never given thought to.

God has a soul.

Hear it once again. God has a soul.

Sounds preposterous doesn't it? It may go against everything you've ever thought or been taught. Maybe, like me, you've never heard of this before or even imagined for a moment about it. It's a truth that will change you, challenge you and excel you, if you will allow it to.

We see this prevailing truth throughout Scripture, from beginning to end. Listen to just a few.

In speaking of Himself concerning His Son God says this: *Behold, My Servant, whom I uphold; My chosen one in whom My **soul** delights* (Isaiah 42:1 and Matthew 12:18).

In I Samuel 2:35 God says: *I will raise up for Myself a faithful priest who will do according to what is in My heart and in My **soul**…*

Job 23:13 declares this truth concerning God: *But He is unique and who can turn Him? And what His **soul** desires, that He does.*

In John 12:27, Jesus spoke these words on the night of His arrest: *Now My **soul** has become troubled.*

How easily the eye overlooks this invading and undeniable truth upon the pages, evading our line of sight. Because God has a soul, we have a soul. We were created in His image. Before you lay this book down, remember what the word soul means. The seat of emotion, desires and appetites, the life, mind and will of a person. The soul is eternal.

God is eternal. His soul has never had a beginning point. He has always been and will always be. He has life, a mind, a will, emotions and desires. And in His eternal image and likeness, you and I were made.

This understanding is the beginning of living, truly living, for each one of us. In the very bed of the womb of life, God fashioned, and formed you and me, just as He did baby Stella. His soul engaged and invested in you and me from the onset. He made you to belong to Him.

It does not matter the circumstances under which your life was conceived, God took over from there. Man's work stopped, and God's soul work began. His soul hedging you about in the pinions of His wings and there, in the shadow of unfailing providence and mastery, He skillfully wrought you in the depths of unconditional love.

You are His soul work.

At the time of conception (your conception), the Heavenly Father took the stretch of His arms of power and encircled the soul round about. From the North and South, to the East and West of your coming forth, there would be no direction in the womb that the Creator could not be seen or felt. Before the eyes could see, He was seen. Before the heart's first beat, the heart of the Almighty pulsated within.

The soul is known by God first and God is the first known by the soul. In your beginning, it was just you and Him. No eye had seen, nor any heart known all that He had planned for you from the very onset of your existence. No one knows you like the Soul Maker.

There is nothing about you that has ever been, or ever will be hidden from His view. It will never matter if anyone else "gets you", God does. He knows you fully. The very hairs on your hair are numbered. He numbered your days before there was even one in place and before you speak a word, He knows what you're going to say.

God does His most intimate and paramount of works, soul to soul. He interlaces a thousand beautiful stories into the fabric of our soul. Stories of Him, His mercy, His unfathomable power, love and untold grace. He is not a superficial God who sets out to work on the surface or outer appearance.

He is a laborer of the soul…your soul and mine. His work is deep and penetrating, encompassing the whole of who we are. God works from the inside out.

In the womb of your birth mother, a grand working takes place. The life He intends to come forth is wrought when His soul lays hold of the soul of His child without interference, unrivaled and without distraction. In the darkness of the womb, His soul is the only light that is needed for new life to come forth. … A truth the soul will desperately need to know and remember as it treks through the seasons of life.

What does this tell us?

There is life before and beyond the breath that fills the lungs. You were alive to Him before you were alive to anyone else. He is your source of life not people, not possessions, not positions, and not condition. Under His hand of power, your soul responds, bends and yields.

Why?

Because He is the Creator or known in Hebrew as, *"Elohim"*. This is the name you and I must remember, know and be known by. Elohim is the first name or word used for God in Scripture.

This is how God introduces Himself to us in His Word, because it is how we first came to know Him. Genesis 1:1 tells us, *In the beginning God (Elohim) created the heavens and the earth.* It is at this line of truth that you and I must step up to and in profession of faith launch out into life. We start at this beginning point with God because this is where your soul found its birthing ground.

What does this mean to us?

Elohim speaks of God as supreme, all powerful and mighty. He set Himself, from the very beginning, to be your source, your hero, your power…your everything. He established that in Him alone, all your needs are found to be supplied.

The apostle Paul wrote: "*And my God shall supply all your needs according to His riches in glory* (Philippians 4:19)." This speaks of not only our physical needs, but the needs of the soul as well. *"All your needs"* are met in God.

When we acknowledge God as Elohim, the soul comes to a place where fullness of living is discovered. Life comes forth as He intended when we bow the knee of worship and acknowledgement before the Soul Maker. Until this reverence of surrender takes place, the soul will wander aimlessly throughout its days, yearning to know its purpose and source of life.

There is a deep longing of the human soul to know and to be known by God. It does not matter what others may tell you or even what you may have told yourself, your soul has the need for intimacy with your Creator. It longs to yield to Him, allowing His mastery to mold and make you into what His heart desires; a process your soul is already familiar with.

Ezekiel 18:4 says this of God; *"Behold, all souls are mine."* No matter how convincing philosophies or worldly wisdom may be in trying to dissuade your soul to believe otherwise, from its depths, the soul will know it is a lie. It has been branded with the truth of God's position and presence.

Even when a confession cannot find its place upon the tongue to this prevailing truth, the cry of the soul will always be to acknowledge it.

The soul cannot escape the cavern of God's existence which has been hollowed out within it. If you calm the soul long enough, silencing the noise of the world, the stillness of the mind will summon what the soul has lost in the distractions and bitter waters of life. Quiet the mind, and the soul will speak. *Be still and know that I am God...and I will be exalted in the earth* (Psalm 46:10 KJV).

A.J. Lauless said, *My soul is too deep to be explore by those who always swam in the shallow end.* The depth of the soul, no one can plummet but God Himself. He carved out an entity of holding so vast, that no human hand could ever fill, because it was meant for Him. Speak this truth out loud for your soul to hear:

He is your deepest desire

Your first love

The longing that no one can fill but Him.

It does not matter how grand or even satisfying, no human love can fill the place that belongs to God.

He is your soul's cry.

My soul is from elsewhere I'm sure of that and I intend to return there.

———

RUMI

CHAPTER THREE

A LONGING FOR HOME

Most are no stranger to pain and loss. Sufferings have left their mark upon all of our lives at some point. At times, we've all probably wondered when exactly it was that grief took hold of our hand in companionship. When the storm clouds gather over our lives, it's not because our soul summoned them to rise and overshadow all we hold dear. They come without warning and apart from invitation. It needs no introduction, nor does it need our permission.

Draped with the cloak of cruelty, losses pierce like a dagger in our beating hearts. Especially when loss comes through the agency of death. When the heart of someone we love ceases to beat, ours never seems to beat the same again. Death falls upon us like night, enveloping our lives, overtaking our very soul in a total eclipse of life. Although still beating, the heart now pulsates with sounds of anguish rather than life. How heavy the soul that has known deep loss.

One of my dearest friends in this world, Melissa, lost both of her grown children (sons), two grandchildren and a daughter-in-law, in a small plane crash just a few days before Christmas. The two brothers were headed to Texas to spend Christmas together with their families. Even though 6 years have passed, to pen the account is a struggle for this writer. There are no words to be found in the human vocabulary. None that can adequately depict the depth of pain and darkness of that event.

When we love another completely, like a parent for their child, what are we to do with all the love we have for them when they are no longer there to receive it? Where is the soul to pour out such monumental love?

It is a most desperate place for any who find themselves cast upon such grievous ground. I've witnessed such ashen earth roll itself out as a bed of sorrow, beneath the life of my friend.

How can the anguish of the human soul find a lodging place upon paper?

How can it bear the weight of it?

What word can we summon to write of a heart utterly shattered?

If tears were the ink, and paper the pain, the two would fail to translate such unspeakable loss. Nothing forged by human hand can hold the grievances of the soul.

My precious friend lives with the loss and separation every minute of every day of her life. The loss goes nowhere. The soul cannot erase such sorrow from its memory. It feels, it hurts, it remembers, and it carries.

The soul cannot escape what it knows. It is unable to part from the events of life as to unbind itself from the knowledge of it. When it is unbearable and beyond its own strength to endure, it will shut down and seek reprieve. Even if it has to retreat outside the confines of reality.

The Psalmist alludes to the existence of this place when he writes: *I would have despaired unless I had believed that I would see the goodness of the LORD in the land of the living.* (Psalm 27:13)

Melissa would often say that she felt like she was standing right at the edge of a very high cliff. With one step in the wrong direction, she feared she would fall and never recover.

Why do we wrestle with acceptance of death?

Why is death so unbearable for the human soul to endure?

These are questions that many of us, no doubt, have asked or pondered over. While we will never have all the answers this side of Heaven, there is an understanding that can unlock the shackles of our pain, allowing the soul to be freed from the weight of it.

Jesus taught: *If you abide in My word, then you are truly disciples of Mine; and you shall know the truth, and the truth shall make you free* (John 8:31,32).

There is an exhortation from the Lord to continue in His word, because truth has great power in the life of one who is bound. When God's Word is present within our lives, truth becomes the key for our bondages. Even the chain of loss that has bound us from the land of the living.

Hear this; *If truth frees then a lie binds.*

Since the beginning of time, the father of lies (Satan), has set his aim to deceive the souls of mankind. He speaks lie after lie, because he wants to keep us from truth. He wants to bind us with lies. These lies link together, forming the very chains of our bondages.

This is what we set our sights on now; truth. Truth about your soul and every other soul that has been created. God's design of the soul is unique and unchanging, even from the beginning. It was not made to know death, to know separation, pain or loss.

As with sickness and suffering, death is not accepted by the soul naturally, because it was not designed to do so. The soul is unending. It will always struggle internally with these things because these things were never in the perfect will of God from the beginning.

The soul was made to fulfill His perfect will.

Hear truth…let truth speak without rival to your soul. From the very beginning of time, God established the perfect world with all the soul would ever need. It had unbroken communion with

Him. There was no sickness, no pain, no harmful thing. Death did not exist, neither did sin or corruption.

The earth was beautiful in every way. Hate, violence, lust, lying, envy, strife, murder, war, dissensions, abuse and any form of perversion or darkness was unknown.

This was and is the faultless plan of God for the soul to thrive and live. God did not fashion the soul of man with death in mind. Death was never in the plan of God. He instituted a boundary to keep death from ever being allowed to enter into the life of His child or, into His world. Genesis chapter one lays this out for us in great detail.

God never brought forth death. In the very good of God, death is never present. Goodbye was never written into your vocabulary by Him. You were never to know separation from those you love or from God.

God is not to blame, although we like to try and give Him the credit. It was mankind that opened the door for all these things to come in by taking of the forbidden. In Genesis chapter three, Eve was tempted by the devil to take of the forbidden. She took and then gave to her husband Adam and he also ate with her. There was a union of soul in the taking. Although there were many consequences to this decision, perhaps the most painful for Adam and Eve was separation from God.

There was a painful fall out from their decision to disobey God.

In Genesis 3:23 we're told; *God drove them out of the garden.* This separation from God would be passed down from them to every other life to follow, including yours and mine. Adam and Eve discovered this pain in their adult years, having to live with the memory of what it was like to walk with God in the cool of the day. They knew all too well what they had lost. Their children would never know of this reality.

We all live with this separation everyday of our lives. Unlike Adam and Eve, ours begins in the delivery room. What God lost with His child out in the world, in the Garden of Eden, He re-establishes in the womb. God instills the level of His relationship and His position, even if only for a brief time. He refuses to leave the soul to itself, even though He knows we will take of the forbidden too.

In this consecrated place, He has instilled something far more commanding than the desire for the forbidden. Far greater than any failure or lineage. It's the greatest start in life any of us can ever have. And we all have been given it.

It cannot be stolen, lost or sold. We cannot escape from its existence. And no matter what the world of science, medicine, philosophy or religious opinion try to dictate or prove; all life is held captive by this undying encounter with the Living God. It is forever embossed with His companionship.

Let us paint out this undying encounter, this certainty for the eye to see. Allow the colors of this pallet of absolute to surface so vividly upon the painting of your understanding, that you get lost in the scope of it. Catch a glimpse of the grand view of God's unexpected artwork of all life. He is the master artisan.

When a soul is born, when that first cry comes forth, it is far more than just a life coming into the world. The nearness and intimacy, that the soul had with God in the womb, came to an abrupt halt. In the womb, there was nothing to challenge or contend with the communion we had between our soul and His. There was a time when it was just you and Him. You were fully His. He had your undivided attention.

But birth changed everything.

The noise of the outside world came flooding in like a monsoon of chaos and opposition. There would now be many voices speaking, other sounds and cries to divert the ear away from the Creator.

Immediately, when the soul is born into the world, it encounters conflict. The place it has known for its life source, its communion with God, His peace, rest, security, love and oneness, has been lost. From the draw of first breath in the land of the living, the soul is in need. It is swaddled in desperation as soon as human hands bring it forth.

The soul is born fractured.

The need to be with its Creator, in unbroken communion and unobstructed view, comes crashing down upon it. A relationship where He is the soul's focus and only source of life, will be its pursuit from day one. The union it once had with its Creator has now been altered and it will never be fulfilled until it resumes this unbroken relationship it was destined to have.

A soul ripped from the arms of God will remain in agony, until it comes to rest in them once again. We weren't the only ones who lost intimacy at birth. God did as well. The Creator's soul agonizes for the soul of His child.

Listen to the anguish of God concerning His children in Hosea 11:8. He's speaking of His children.

> *How can I give you up, Oh Ephraim? (Israel) How*
> *can I surrender you, Oh Israel? ... My heart is turned over*
> *within Me. All My compassions are kindled.*

God's Soul was the first to cry out in creation. When a soul is born, God has lost the intimacy that He longs to have, that He created His child to know and capture as a way of life. His heart mourns the separation of His child. What a difficult and painful experience to let go of your child, to share them with the world.

This was your soul's first goodbye.

Although our unformed substance would not be able to put to memory its initial beginning with God, the soul was imprinted with the indelible knowledge of His existence, His nearness and presence. Because you were inscribed into Him. Oh, how I pray you will hear the words of Isaiah 49:15,16:

> *Can a woman forget her nursing child, and have no compassion on the son of her womb? Even these may forget, but I will not forget you. Behold, I have inscribed you on the palms of My hands; Your walls are continually before Me.*

The word *"inscribe"* in this verse is steeped in rich connotation for us. It means to carve out or engrave upon stone or metal a law or a decree. It speaks of a permanence, of a governing rule that is never to be changed or rewritten. This word turns loudly with such beauty; affirming for us the undying and undeniable love that God has for the soul of His child.

It peels back the layer of our very existence. The soul would forever conceive in its depth, that it belongs with and belongs to the One who is unseen but not unknown.

Jeremiah 31:3 also proclaims the heart of God for us saying: *The LORD appeared to him from afar, saying, 'I have loved you with an everlasting love; Therefore, I have drawn you with lovingkindness.'*

Your love story did not begin with one who is clothed with flesh and blood. It began with Him, the lover and keeper of your soul. He set His affections upon you before you even understood what love was.

He is the initiator of this vast and inescapable attribute. A love story written by Him. You were first loved by Him and that love has never been absent from your life, not for a minute of any day. Not even in your life's darkest hour.

Every soul has this watermark embossed upon it in the womb. It is forever engraved with God's mark of love and infallible work. These things are embedded in the marrow of the soul so one day, when the time is right, it will return from whence it came. Your soul belongs with God. If settled long enough from the clamoring of life, it will know and remember.

Hear the words of Psalm 42:1-2: ... *As the deer pants for the water brooks, so my soul pants for You, O God. My soul thirsts for God, for the living God; when shall I come and appear before God?*

The soul is thirsty because it began this way. It languishes in desperation for the Heavenly Father. Even when the flesh does not know what it is feverishly in search of, the soul has not forgotten. It is secured within.

It cries out to be heard, to be followed, for it knows where it must go. There is a holy compass installed within, pointing the way, drawing and tugging the heart strings saying, ...*this is the way, walk in it* (Isaiah 30:21).

The soul has an eternal home and there, in this unseen place of immense perfection and untold beauty, God is waiting. He is anticipating the soul's homecoming.

Hear once again the soul's cry of the beloved found in Psalm 63:1: *...Oh God, Thou art my God; I shall seek Thee earnestly; My soul thirst for Thee, my flesh yearns for Thee, in a dry and weary land where there is not water.*

What torment is entrenched in the Psalmist words. The pulsating of despair is heard with every beat of his longing heart. He understood the greatest and most desperate need of his life. There is a thirst of soul so deep, and necessary for living, that only God Himself can satisfy. Until the soul comes to this reality, that it is in search of God, that God is what it yearns and aches for, it will have no rest.

Longing for the Living God, the soul seeks to know when it can come home, home to Him. Many, search their entire lives, trying to learn what it is they must find. This quest has often led many to try and fill their greatest need with people, ungodly relationships, lustful living, drugs, alcohol, material possessions, and earthly positions of power, greedy motivations, perfect physiques, people pleasing, cults and more.

To seek life, apart from God, is wasteful foraging upon the plains of the earth, which will never meet this overwhelming need of the soul. Searching souls can be found on a massive and worldwide level. None of us are immune from needing the Living God, no matter what our chosen beliefs may be. The irresistible and despairing need for God remains.

Hunter Thompson was such a soul. He was an American Journalist who was known for his provocative and flamboyant writing style. Listen to a line he penned out of the desperation of his own soul: *All my life my heart has sought what it cannot name.*

On February 20th, 2005, it is believed that he took his own life. There are countless souls just like him; thirsty, yearning, desperate and lost.

The prophet Isaiah wrote: *We have waited for Thee eagerly; Thy name, even Thy memory, is the desire of our souls. At night, my soul longs for Thee, indeed, my spirit within me seeks Thee diligently* (Isaiah 26:8-9).

Every soul is born homesick.

Burrowed deep in the heart of each of us is the greatest need of all: to return to God. To come home to Him. To find life in Him and in Him alone. This is the greatest need of the human soul, and God placed it there before you ever took your first breath. Even when the soul forgets, this truth remains, unaltered and anchored firmly in place as God intended it to be.

Listen to the anguish of the apostle Paul's heart concerning this same truth in Philippians 1:23: *But I am hard-pressed from both directions, having the desire to depart and be with Christ, for that is very much better.*

Paul was "hard pressed". There was an agony of soul to go home.

Not his earthly home, but his heavenly, eternal home. His soul boldly, with fullness of hope, declared that it was a stranger passing through. Heaven was his home and this life was but a journey to get there. Fixing his eyes on Heaven, Paul's soul charted its course and never looked back. Heaven becomes the wind in your sails, when you place your faith in the truth of it. The soul knows that God is there and it will stop at nothing to get to Him.

Looking back to the saints of old, all the way back to the Old Testament times, the author of the book of Hebrews lets us in on their spiritual secret to living by faith (Hebrews 11:13-16).

> *All these died in faith, without receiving the promises,*
> *but having seen them and having welcomed*
> *them from a distance, and having confessed that they*
> *were strangers and exiles on the earth.*
>
> *For those who say such things make it clear that they are*
> *seeking a country of their own.*
>
> *And indeed, if they had been thinking of that*
> *country from which they went out, they would have*
> *had opportunity to return.*
>
> *But as it is, they desire a better country, that is, a*
> *heavenly one. Therefore, God is not ashamed to be called their*
> *God; for He has prepared a city for them.*

From the day your God saw you off into the world, He began preparing for your return. He numbered the days until you could come back to Him. He's anticipated and even longed for your arrival, even before you left Him. You, dear soul, have His heart completely. It is this love that gives your soul its immeasurable worth. Nothing else.

During Jesus short stay upon this earth, He encountered believers and doubters; supporters and enemies. One day, Jesus went into the temple to teach the crowd about Him. There was a group of Pharisees who brought a woman caught in adultery and threw her down on the dusty ground before Him. Intending on trapping Jesus in an awkward situation, they began quoting the book of the Law. They wanted her stoned, but Jesus wanted her forgiven.

He has a way of reaching down into the gut of the soul. Having asked the one without sin to cast the first stone, her accusers began to walk off one by one. Jesus forgives this woman with such compassion. Afterwards, this is what Jesus says, even as some of the Pharisees continue to linger within ear shot of His voice (John 8:12-14):

> *I am the Light of the world; he who follows*
> *Me will not walk in the darkness but will have the Light*
> *of life. So, the Pharisees said to Him, 'You are testifying*
> *about Yourself; Your testimony is not true'*
>
> *Jesus answered and said to them, 'Even if I testify*
> *about Myself, My testimony is true, for I know where*
> *I came from and where I am going; but you do not know*
> *where I come from or where I am going.*

Jesus' authenticity was based upon where He came from and where He was going. This is what testifies of the soul's purpose and establishes who it is. This is very powerful. When the soul knows where it came from and where it is going, it then can call Heaven and Earth to testify on its behalf. God has placed this instinct within. It is undeniably Him.

A PLACE CALLED HOME –

In late summer, the migration of the monarch butterfly occurs. If you're in the right place at the right time, you can see hundreds of them clinging to tree limbs and shrubbery as the flock journeys to a remote mountain site in central Mexico.

Scientists have found 16 of these sites, ranging from one to ten acres each, within a 100-mile radius, where millions of butterflies from North America spend the winter.

No one knows how butterflies find their way there. Each generation that migrates is new and has never been there before. Yet something programmed into their tiny bodies directs them to a place they have never seen, but is a home they instinctively know they must find.
-Lettie Cowman, Springs in the Valley

Knowing your origin is the gateway to your God given destiny. It all begins here. This beginning point is everything to your soul. It testifies of your ending, ordering your steps to Heaven, and drawing you homeward.

Although Rumi, the Muslim Poet had the destination wrong, among other things, there is truth found in his statement: *My soul is from elsewhere, I'm sure of that. I intend to end up there.* Even when the soul is lost in the darkness of manmade religion, it is driven within to find home.

No matter what our chosen belief is, our soul understands instinctively, that it does not belong here. Hidden, deep within the soul, is the longing to return to God. The One True Living God. In the chromosome of your makeup, God placed this unceasing drive.

Have you ever asked your soul what it longs for? Have you ever stopped long enough to shut out every other voice of intrusion and influence, opinion, philosophy, pride, anger, prejudice, opportunity, hate, and fear, long enough to listen for the answer you've been longing to know?

From Him you came and to Him you will return.

The soul was designed to remember the eternal.

Until my soul connected with Yours, how could
I have known I was in search of You

———

BLACKBIRD

CHAPTER FOUR

THE SOUL IN NEED

The conference began on time, the ladies had gathered together in great anticipation of what the guest speaker would say. What message had the Lord given to her for all of us? Great excitement enthralled the group and finally the speaker stepped to the platform. She was there to tell of her soul's journey with God.

As she began, from the very first word of her message, you could feel God fall into our very atmosphere. Such speakers are extremely rare in the women's event arena. I frequent these circles and as I sat there, I knew we had God's woman for such a time as this. There was no hype, no jokes to break the ice, no anecdotes given…only God.

Straight as an arrow she stood and with great resolve spilled out a story so imposing in scope and reach, that instantly our attention settled in, thirsty for every word. Her loss was inconceivable. On many levels, her family suffered; more than any other I had ever heard.

In describing the trying time that assailed the life she knew; her words still linger upon my heart. In paraphrasing, this is the heartbeat of what she said:

A cataclysmic event roared upon the shores of our perfect lives and when it hit the land of our living, nothing would ever be the same. As morning finally rose upon our pain and suffering, I surveyed our family, our life and took a good hard look at what remained. I thought my heart would surely stop beating. In that viewing, the life we once had was utterly unrecognizable. The storm had destroyed everything. I did not even recognize my own life anymore.

She did not look for empathy or comfort; only to speak of the unfailing hand of God to bring a soul through the storms of life. With God, it's always about what's on the other side of the pain, not in the moment of suffering at hand. Just beyond that valley, on the other side of that mountain, across that impossible passage, awaits what only God can see. He is the God of immeasurably more.

This is true for every one of us…everyone of us.

There are many such stories and tragedies intertwined through the canon of Scripture that bear witness for us today. God has placed them there for us, memorializing the human soul and the constant fight of surrender. Page after page, line after line, telling of the desperate hours that fell upon the lives of God's people. Times of great threat, agony, cost and the misery that consequences can usher in. Decisions that became the very current of one's life, giving bend and sway to the course they would take.

Their torrents become a tutorial for us; winding through the water veins of their penalties, exposing the weakness of the one, that it might give strength to the many. Besieged souls, powerless to control or paddle their way to the riverbank of escape. Such stories imprinted into the eternal pages of God's Word that we may know and draw from.

Our struggles become mighty platforms if we are courageous enough to allow transparency to take up the microphone. There is nothing more beautiful or impactful, than a life that has clothed itself with unassuming bravery and steps out of the shadows of failure to declare ... *Come and hear, all who fear God, and I will tell of what He has done for my soul. (Psalm 66:16)* Failure is not a person, it is an event; an event of influence if given the opportunity.

One such event is that of a little prophet by the name of Jonah. There was no soul more despairing for God's help in his hour of great need than Jonah. Most people are somewhat familiar with his saga: The tale of the man who was swallowed by a whale. A soul who ran from God and lived to tell about it.

It's ironic how our defiance to run away from the will of God will be the very wheel of pain that turns us around. This was the situation Jonah found himself in. Having received an assignment from God, he fled. Jonah hopped a ship, trying to sail away from Heaven's plan for his life. As he would soon discover, there are no waters deep enough to hide the rebellious soul. Jonah's escape route from God's will is what ended up being a detour to obedience; the hard way.

Running away from Heaven's will, he found himself sinking headlong into the center of it. His refusal took him in the opposite direction of where he had intended to go. Only it took a whale to do it. Defiance is but a woodshed of discipline waiting for our entry. And enter he did.

God's catalyst for change will take on many forms. You may have never experienced a ride in a whale, but no doubt, something beyond your control has taken you in a direction you were trying to avoid. Defiance will never lead to peace, but it will lead to pain. Some are more painful and costly than others.

Disobedience is a storm of our own making. It will toss us around in the turmoil of our waywardness until our white flag of surrender is raised, even if it's from the depths of a whale belly. The mercy of God, even in the deepest pit of insolence, can reach the backslidden and redirect a soul on the run. Our rebellion can never hide us from the eyes of grace.

Jonah's situation was dire, dark and utterly desperate. I can't imagine a more difficult place to be than in the stomach of a great sea monster. The imagination fails to bring it to realization. But we can quiet our hearts before the pages of Scripture, and agony of Jonah, as he describes for us in detail what it was like.

Listen to the account of his time spent in the gut of that great beast on assignment. (Jonah 2:3 & 5)

For You had cast me into the deep, Into the heart of the seas, and the current engulfed me. All Your breakers and billows passed over me.

Water encompassed me to the point of death. The great deep engulfed me, Weeds were wrapped around my head.

I descended to the roots of the mountains. The earth with its bars was around me forever.

Jonah was in a dark and trying place, fully engulfed in the consequences of his decisions. The lowest of places one can find themselves. A dwelling where death was certain, and all was lost. There was no human hand of assistance accessible; no power on earth at his disposal nor none strong enough to order his release. Help for him in the darkness of utter gloom was outside of his reach.

There is no position on earth lonelier than that of knowing you are wrong and having no recourse to make it right: There is no greater despair of soul than to reach for a hand to help and find none to lay hold. When the soul sinks to such a lodging where flesh and blood cannot reach to save, a God greater than one's hopelessness must step in if salvation is to come. Jonah needed someone stronger than his whale of suffering.

The only One Jonah had to call on was God. The very One he was trying to evade, he now sought to find. Defiance carves a path of desperation, leading us back around to face the same mission we fought so hard to reject. The soul in such a place is abandoned to the clemency of God.

There is only One who can rescue, there is only one answer given; His answer. Jonah's soul cry ascended from his place of overwhelming need and all he could do was wait for Heaven's reply.

Had God forgotten him there? Would God be able to reach him, hear him and see him in the depth of such a place? Does God remember the name of the wayward or does He blot it out before His eyes?

Some years ago, I was making a hospital visit to see a woman who lived across the street from me at the time. She had suffered from a brain bleed and the prognosis was grim. I and a friend went to pray over her and her family. We had been privileged to lead this dear lady to Jesus just a year previous at a Bible Study. But her grown children needed to know about Jesus; A burden that she had carried in prayer for some time.

In and out of jail, they were hopelessly lost to a world of drugs, crime and chaos. Much like Jonah, they were running from God. God would use their mother's condition to confront their hard realities. As we walked into the ICU, we knew that she didn't have long. She lay there in a coma and on life support. Her children were not present when we arrived.

Draped across her chest was a cross necklace and an open Bible with a piece of paper bearing the name of my precious neighbor. Her name was written with big letters in red ink as if to ensure that it would be seen. Why would her name need to be placed there? We both wondered about this at the time.

We prayed over her, leaning in to whisper our goodbyes, *See you when we get there sweet friend.* On the way out of the hospital, we ran into her two sons who were headed in. They were emotionally shaken and understandably heartbroken. Her oldest son told us how anxious they were for God to hear their prayers and to heal their mom.

He went on to explain that they wanted God to know who their mother was, so they wrote her name for Him to see. The younger of the two added, *And we wrote her name in big red letters to be sure God would see it.*

These young men did not know if God knew who their mother was, so they wrote out her name and placed it on her, there in the ICU. It was a dagger to my heart to see the face of living hopelessness before me. It was their soul's cry in the only way they knew to give it. Somehow, their soul understood to reach out to God in Heaven. Though they did not know God, their soul reached back into its hidden treasure of understanding and called out to Him. It was in the DNA of who they were.

The prophet Jeremiah declared for us: …*You know me, O LORD;*

You see me... (Jeremiah 12:3) He not only sees us, He knows us by name. (John 10:3)

Sin, no matter how long, how deep or how rebellious, can never erase our name before God. It can never remove or blot out our existence in the eyes of the LORD. There is no place where we may find ourselves that God does not know us, or that He cannot see us. Jonah's cry rose from the belly of a whale in the depth of the ocean. And even in such a place as this, God heard him.

> Hear the soul cry of Jonah: *Then Jonah prayed to the LORD his God from the stomach of the fish, and he said, I called out of my distress to the LORD, And He answered me. I cried for help from the depth of Sheol; You heard my voice.* Jonah 2:1-2

This cry is Jonah's testimony of God in his time of need. Jonah's soul cried out to the Living God and He heard him. He didn't have to tell God who he was. His cry was all God needed to identify that it was him. Jonah's soul, even when the body was on the brink of death, defaulted to what it knew to do...

Cry out.

We all speak this dialect of desperation. And the powerful understanding is this: no name is ever needed to be given. The soul's cry is unique to itself. No one speaks your soul cry but you. A soul's cry is everything. Heaven identifies your call.

Jonah did not have the luxury of an offering to give, or time to make atonement for his wrongs. There was no phone call to be made, no opportunity to seek counsel, support, or the prayers of others who might storm the gates of Heaven on his behalf. Being put on the prayer list at church was not an option! There was no visit to be made by the Pastor, no holy altar to approach for mercy, and no sacrifice he could make on his behalf.

In this hour of overwhelming crisis, the stomach of that whale became Jonah's altar of repentance; his meeting place with God. Heaven wasn't waiting for a doctrinally correct prayer, not even a lengthy prayer quoting Scripture or claiming the promises of God. Heaven wasn't looking for faith, and it sought for no assurances to be made. Only one thing Heaven was attentive to. Only one sound it bent low to hear in the deepness of the sea.

Jonah's soul cry... the cry that is felt, poured out upon the altar of surrender. The sound that billows from within the mighty breakers of God, washing over our dark condition.

There are others in God's Word who found themselves facing their altars of defeat. For Paul, it was a dusty road on the way to Damascus. For Moses, a burning bush, for Elijah it was a cave, and for Peter, a boat. This is what we must know and remember, no matter where we may find ourselves:

God longs to invade our desperations.

The great collision of Heaven's grace with the tormented soul. Life's most beautiful altars are raised in the belly of our hardest and lowest places. In the unreachable and unchangeable circumstances. And there, as we sink and spiral downward into the depths of life's forsaken and diminishing place, Heaven is purposefully constructing an altar of praise at the bottom; just in time for our arrival.

The cry raised from such a far and distant place of darkness and pain, is the sweetest offering a soul can lay upon the altar found there. Jonah made an offering that no one else could have made for him. He laid himself upon the altar of anguish and surrendered all he had at that moment to give…his life. It's a sacrifice that only he could make.

Sometimes it's not because of a needed correction that we visit such places against our will as was Jonah's case. Many times, they are God's greatest gifts to us, wrapped up in a package of appointed suffering. It may have been seemingly by the hands of others or circumstances beyond our control. It does not matter the avenue upon which we arrived at our great hour of challenge; these are only catalysts appointed for change. The Giver is waiting, longing to release something greater and grander into the very heartbeat of our life.

Let your soul know and receive this God given certainty: *Every trial does not come with an altar…every trial is an altar.*

The soul that has come face to face with such, has been summoned to a cross; a mount where God will and can exalt Jesus before the eyes of the world upon our ordained tree of suffering. It may not seem like it at the onset, but such places are not commanded by human hands. They are ordained by the great Carpenter Himself.

Wherever you are, God stands ready to hear your soul's cry. Even if there is none to hear your cry but you. Raise it still. Raise it loud and intentional. There is One who stands ready to answer. No matter how low you have sunk. Change is not required in order to be heard. How that bears repeating...***change is not required in order to be heard.***

No doubt, Jonah would have sung this Psalm in praise once he arrived on the shore: *Had it not been the LORD who was on our side, when men rose up against us, ... ⁴Then the waters would have engulfed us, the stream would have swept over our soul;* (Psalm 124:2 ,4)

He's waiting for intentional surrender. And when that cry of utter abandon to His will is heard, God takes the lyrics of our submission and orchestrates an untold hymn of amazing grace.

There is no perfection, only beautiful versions of brokenness

———

SUSAN ALDER, AUTHOR

CHAPTER FIVE

AN ANCHOR FOR THE SOUL

A story is told of a shipwreck that occurred some time ago, deep in the Pacific Ocean. Without warning, a fierce gale rose up on the sea, engulfing the tiny vessel in its presence. The captain and crew were caught completely off guard. After hours of battling the unrelenting waves, hammering against the side of the ship, the crew had no choice but to throw themselves overboard if they were to survive. But the height of the waves proved to be too much on the crew and all but one succumbed to the ocean's force.

Out of 24 crewmen, only one had made it through the night in the raging waters. Just before going under, the ship's captain was able to send out an SOS call for help. As soon as there was a window of opportunity, crews were sent out to search for and rescue any survivors. With the challenge of the unpredictable, and at times volatile weather still churning out in the ocean, they looked for days with no avail. Pieces of the wreckage could be seen floating in the area where the ship was believed to have gone under. But still no life was spotted.

Finally, after 8 days of an exhaustive search effort, one of the rescue ships spotted a man clinging to the top of a rock, about a mile off the coastline of a nearby island. They labored to get the man aboard. Half dead and in need of much rest, it was a couple of days before the man was conscious and able to talk to the authorities. When asked how he had survived through the storm the man replied:

"I was washed into these rocks and was able to climb up on one of them. No matter how hard the waves crashed against me, no matter how hard the wind blew; the rock never moved."

This sailor had found a rock in the midst of his storm; a refuge and bulwark in the raging sea. He found a place that was immoveable and could not be overcome, even in the face of a storm that held him powerless. We need a stronger place, a safety in the heart of our danger and peril if we are to endure through the ramparts of life. Sometimes we are cast upon them in an hour of crisis, beyond our own planning and ability to weather.

King David was a man of many failures, yet upon his brow sat the crown of Israel. His robe of royalty and favor was not something David earned or obtained the right to receive, it was solely because of God's choosing. Scripture tells us that it was not because David was the greatest, or even the first in his father's house, quite the contrary. He was the least of all. He's described as "ruddy and handsome"

The Israeli King was a fierce enemy upon the battlefield. He was fearless in the face of his enemies, even when they were giants and he had nothing but a handful of stones drawn from the river bed as his weapon. David never wavered in war, even if he was out-numbered. It made no difference to David, he trusted in God fully.

Listen to the testimony of this trusting Psalmist. Psalm 57:2:

> *I will cry to God Most High who accomplishes all things
> for me. In Psalm 25:1, he goes on to say: To You O
> LORD, I lift up my soul. Again, in Psalm 77:1 he declares:
> My voice rises to God and I will cry aloud. My voice
> rises to God and He will hear me.*

God knows our unspoken struggles, our internal conflicts and hidden hurt. Even those aches so deep that no word can articulate, those wordless grievances His ear captures as valuable and worthy of response. In times of despair and burdensome sorrow, the soul must look to the love of God. Leaning into all that He is, falling full weight into the unfailing and everlasting love of Heaven. *It has been said that true love causes the soul to crawl out of its hiding place.*

Oftentimes, we abandon our faith in the face of trying situations because we have not yet grasped the unceasing and immeasurable power wrapped up in the eternal love of God. What cannot be understood or explained this side of Heaven, must be laid hold of in faith. Faith alone. Nothing can conquer or overtake the love of God. It is fierce and unrelenting.

Listen to these verses that give us a glimpse of this commanding truth:

> *For I am convinced that neither death, nor life, nor angels,*
> *nor principalities, nor things present, nor things to come,*
> *nor powers, nor height, nor depth, nor any other created thing,*
> *will be able to separate us from the love of God, which*
> *is in Christ Jesus our Lord.* Romans 8:38-39

The apostle Paul, the penman in this passage, is very specific in conveying his stand on the love of God. He states, unequivocally, that he is convinced of the power of God's love for him. When we look at the deeper meaning of the word *"convinced"*, we find this profound meaning in place: *to rely upon by inward certainty. To agree with, to be assured of, to believe in, have confidence in, to be persuaded of, to trust in or yield to.*

In using this specific and deliberate verbiage, God's servant was making a grand affirmation to God's people saying: *Having an inward certainty, I am fully relying on the love of God. I am persuaded to trust in it and to be confident in it, knowing that I can trust in His love for me, having no fear to yield to its will and way.*

He was absolutely secure in God's love for him. But Paul didn't arrive at this place of confidence overnight. It was a journey of soul, of great peril and unspeakable loss to his own whale of struggle. It wasn't the blessings that had anchored him in the love of Heaven, it had been his trials. He had suffered many things. He describes these times for us when writing to the Church at Corinth, saying:

Five times I received from the Jews thirty-nine lashes. Three times I was beaten with rods, once I was stoned, three times I was shipwrecked, a night and a day I have spent in the deep.

I have been on frequent journeys, in dangers from rivers, dangers from robbers, dangers from my countrymen, dangers from the Gentiles, dangers in the city, dangers in the wilderness, dangers on the sea, dangers among false brethren;

I have been in labor and hardship, through many sleepless nights, in hunger and thirst, often without food, in cold and exposure. 2 Corinthians 11:24-27

The great apostle had walked through many a valley with His God and had could confidently say, God loves me! "His love is all I need", resounds from his soul. When God becomes your soul's cry, your soul will not hesitate to call to Him in the day of trouble. Even when there is no light to be found in the overwhelming darkness of life, the soul is drawn to go farther than it can see: To reach for the unseen, knowing unreservedly, that it is there.

Out of the depths, in full transparency, and apart from human agency, the soul's cry will find no rest until it comes to rest before its Maker. Whatever the need, and wherever the need, God waits for the soul to look up and raise up its battle cry to Heaven. There is no soul beyond His reach or ability to save.

As we discussed earlier, King David understood this great avenue of hope as well. He was a man, who at times, was surrounded by armies, all wanting to take his life and keep him from the rightful rule as King over Israel. Listen to his acknowledgment:

> *I call upon the LORD, who is worthy to be praised, and I am savedfrom my enemies. For the waves of death encompassed me;*

> *The torrents of destruction overwhelmed me; the cords of Sheol surrounded me; The snares of death confronted me.*

> *In my distress, I called upon the LORD, Yes, I cried to my God;*

> *And from His temple He heard my voice, and my cry for help came into His ears.* 2 Samuel 22:4-7

I love the words, *"From His temple He heard my voice and my cry for help came into His ears."* In this time, there was no temple of God built yet upon the earth. David is referring to Heaven, where God's temple was. Heaven cannot be seen by us with the human eye. There is a great gulf of space between us.

What does this mean for us? There is no gulf of separation so great that the soul cannot be heard. This is what David understood and believed about God and His love for him. Just like the apostle Paul. Just like Jonah.

Crying is a way your soul speaks when your mouth can't speak on your behalf; when the groanings are too deep for words. (Romans 8:26) The soul's cry is transmitted on a two-way band of communication. From our lips to Heaven's ears and from Heaven's ears to our altars of trial.

This is the full and unending cycle of hope.

At times we cry over rather than to. Hear that again; sometimes *we cry over our situation rather than to God out of our situation. Heaven is working to speak, longing to reach out but to no avail.*

C.S. Lewis wrote: *The time when there is nothing at all in your soul except a cry for help, may be just that time when God can't give it to you. You are like the drowning man who can't be helped because he clutches and grabs. Perhaps your own reiterated cries deafen you to the voice you hoped to hear.*

How often we exchange our God given right to cry to Him, for the emotional choice to cry over. We must learn the difference.

There are seasons when we must do as Isaac did when he journeyed to Beersheba. Isaac was the promised son to Abraham and Sarah. In Genesis 26, Isaac was surrounded by petty quarrels over the ownership of wells. The enemy will disturb us with petty things that have no weight or bearing on eternity. Small, insignificant worries of life are thorns bent on overtaking our peace. They choke out the life and kill off the good.

Troubles are noise for the soul. They will speak louder than your faith, sweeping your soul into anxiety and alarm. We must unplug the amplifier of its voice so to silence the chaos of our mind just as Isaac did.

Finding himself in such a place, Isaac decided to seek a much-needed solace from such disturbances because they were weighing him down. He does a very wise thing we do well to learn from. He pitched his tent far away from the situation of conflict. Stillness positions us to hear. It removes the noise and chaos from its throne of authority by muting the megaphone of strife. It was this very night that Isaac heard from God. God had a message, a revelation, a confirmation that He wanted to give his servant.

Isaac's internal storm was drowning out the voice of God.

Be still and know, the Psalmist wrote. (Psalm 46:10). Stillness is powerful when the mind is focused upon God. Concerning this, we have an unfailing promise given to us by God: *And He will keep Him in perfect peace whose mind is stayed on thee.* (Isaiah 26:3)

For our soul to have its needs met, it needs someone bigger than itself; larger than its own life and mightier than its struggles and losses. This is learned line by line, day by day, struggle by struggle, and agony by agony. The soul has to be awakened to turn to its Creator; to reunite with His power and abundant life. Sometimes, it takes the loss of all things to awaken the soul to its origin and source of life.

Through many tribulations, we must enter the Kingdom of Heaven (Acts 14:22). There is a painful path carved out for God's child to walk. Until the soul has lost everything, how can God become its everything? Until all is lost, how can He be our all?

God is willing to allow suffering in your life. Not because He is doing something **to you** in these bitter events, but rather, He is doing something **for you**.

Referencing God, the Psalmist says this: *I will rejoice and be glad in Your lovingkindness, Because You have seen my affliction; You have known the troubles of my soul,* (Psalm 31:7). God understands our troubles. He is acquainted with those things that disturb our peace and wall us about in fear and despondency. He sees into our chaos and dives deep into our storm-tossed waters.

He is not after a miraculous rescue. He's after a soul rescue. God is the pursuer of souls, your soul and mine. There isn't a day that passes upon the pages of history that are not marked with the tracks of the Holy Hunter and Divine Companion. When trouble speaks another message into your life and you feel unwanted; that you are unimportant or unvalued; that your struggles are unknown or that God does not care about the plights your soul endures…Your soul can know that is a lie.

These deceptive and defeating thoughts can disorient the soul, causing it to lose its footing in the face of doubt and fear. This is when the battered soul must search out the Rock, climb up upon His anchorage and cling to all He is until the storm subsides. And in that determined hold, the reminders of who you are to Him will speak louder than the waves crashing about you. With every swelling of turbulent water rising above your weary head, and no matter the infinite volume of certain loss that beats against your faith, **He will never move.**

Why?

Because He loves you.

His love is immoveable. His love never runs... it never abandons... and it never surrenders.

There is no wave of destruction that can destroy or remove His love for you. His affections set upon you give your life immeasurable and intrinsic value. Your soul's worth is incalculable. Life's challenges are important to Him because your soul is important to Him.

I love the words preserved for us through the prophet Ezekiel concerning the care God has for His people: *As a shepherd cares for his herd in the day when he is among his scattered sheep, so I will care for My sheep and will deliver them from all the places to which they were scattered on a cloudy and gloomy day.* Ezekiel 34:12

Those cloudy and gloomy days imply storm and sorrow; the places from where God's sheep must be rescued. There's a Native American Proverb that reads: *The soul would have no rainbow if the eyes had no tears."* The rain will come. The storm clouds will gather. Of these, we have no control. Cloudless days are few and far between. Therefore, we need a Shepherd. He will weather the storms with us. Shelter us from the rain and hide us until the clouds pass over and the storm is no more.

God knows that the soul needs to be shepherded. The soul's understanding of this relationship will both secure and deliver, even from the stormy gales of fear and displacement. There can be no counterfeit or replacement for this rapport in the life of the soul. With staff in hand, God dwells within and walks among us. *He leads us beside the still waters, and He restores our soul.* (Psalm 23) And when the terrors of life have caused us to lose our footing, His soul will lead us home.

I have a dear friend who was saved out of a life-long drug addiction. God reached down and radically saved and delivered her. She had two sons but had lost custody of them due to her drug use. Their grandmother was raising them. I watched her grow in the Lord and blossom into this wonderful woman of God. It was a complete and unexplainable transformation! Just how God likes it.

The cry of her heart became that God would save both of her boys. In time, she sensed that God had given her heart an assurance that not one of them would perish, but both would have eternal life. (John 31:16). When her oldest boy was about to enter his senior year of High School, he was involved in a horrific motorcycle accident. The doctors did not believe he would survive.

This was a fatal blow to her heart, as any parent can relate. When she arrived at the hospital, she found him on life support and unresponsive. As the days turned into weeks, she found herself more desperate for God than ever before. She began crying out to God, refusing to let go of the promise He gave her to save her son.

She refused to leave his side during this long ordeal. Day after day, her gaze was fixed upon his vital signs made visible on the machines that were keeping him alive. Whenever the blood pressure or heart rate would drop or increase to an unacceptable degree she did something that has forever impacted my life. Sitting on the edge of his bed, this mother would bend down laying her chest on top of her son and lean into his ears, so he could hear her.

Her words were always the same. *Listen to mama's heartbeat. Feel my lungs breathe in and breathe out. Breathe with me.* Speaking to his heart, she would whisper repeatedly, *beat as one with mine. Listen to the beating of my heart, it will lead you back into the land of the living.*

In time, his vital signs would return to normal range. He responded to her voice. As promised, God did save her son. We can trust Him with that which is most precious to us.

When found in those desperate hours of living, when we feel sure we will never breathe again, let alone return to the land where life is found; we can fall into the arms of our Heavenly Father. Leaning in to all that He is, silences the chaos and noise of the pain beating within us. And there, calling from the shadows of our surrender, the sound of the Almighty can be heard. In the stillness of that conscious rest, beating with perfect sovereignty and hope, the heart of God will bring us back.

This is what God does for His child when they are crippled beneath their circumstances. Like the gentle and caring Shepherd that He is, He bends down to listen, waiting for the cry of the soul to come forth. His reply, in every agony of life, is always the same:

Listen to my heart beat. Bring your beating aching heart close to mine. Hide yourself in Me until there is but one heartbeat heard. Breathe with Me. Hear my voice. It will lead your soul back into the land of the living.

You are His soul's cry. Your soul can trust in Him. He will never abandon you, nor will He ever forsake you. In this understanding, the soul can face down fear of the unknown, because of the One who is known.

His soul will always lead you to life.

Sometimes we are so afraid to ask the important questions in life; not because we fear the wronganswers, but because we fear the truth.

—

STEVEN AITCHISO

CHAPTER SIX

LOVE IS CALLING

As we navigate the waters of life we must fight with determined resolve if we are to lay hold of truth. Swelling from the waters of this battle is the unrelenting fight of the human soul. It's the epic war between truth and lies; both seeking to rule and to be heard above the other. An ancient conflict that assails us all from birth. Such combat, we are all participants in.

The impacts of these strivings, these losses and wins, no life is immune to. We all suffer the casualties and unexpected demands upon this unseen battlefield.

There are no bystanders, no neutral parties. Even if we refuse to participate in or acknowledge the presence of such. We are all in it. Every life, every soul is affected, stirred, swayed and touched by the existence of this great warring of hostilities.

A holy line has been drawn, a declaration of reign established. The boundary between Light and darkness put in place by God before the world was ever brought forth. He has made His stand clear and without wavering, summoned us to join Him there.

The question raised at any given hour is this: what side is our soul on?

Truth is God's fixed and settled reality. It is the absolutes for all life. And it has been settled since the beginning of time. Truth is unalterable.

These absolutes are bombarded daily by the unceasing barrage of unfounded philosophies and incessant debates that materialize from earthly reasoning. Such enemies of truth all have one thing in common; they all make noise. Empty, hollow noise. It's not a noise to deliver, heal, restore, strengthen, improve, help or even sustain let alone save. (The intention is only to be heard; to erect a platform for themselves, driven by blinded ignorance.)Which is the most selfish use of our God given language.

This current generation is no different than the very first one. The world's message remains intact, ringing just as loud today; *"The truth is what I make it…I could set the world on fire and call it rain."* -author unknown

Charles Spurgeon said, *"A lie can travel half way around the world while the truth is putting on its shoes."* Facts may be many, but the truth is one.

Truth will sound like hate for those who hate the truth. Lies are so well established and grounded in our society, and truth so obscured, that when the two converge with one another, right seems wrong and wrong seems right.

Truth is everything. It is the compass for living, the light in the darkness, the way when we are lost, and our anchorage when the storms of life shake our very foundations. Without it, we would be hopelessly lost in this world.

The night that Jesus was arrested, He was taken back and forth between Caiaphas the High Priest and Pontius Pilate, the governor of Rome. As Jesus stood before Pilate, He was asked by the great militant leader, *Are you the King of the Jews*? Upon which Jesus answered,

> *…Thou sayest that I am a king. To this end was I born, and for this cause came I into the world, that I should bear witness unto the truth. Every one that is of the truth heareth my voice. I came to testify of the truth.* John 18:37 KJV

The Lord came to testify of the truth. It helps put the importance of truth into perspective for us. Testifying of the truth would send Jesus to suffer and die a barbaric death. It would cost Him the presence of His home in Heaven and the absence of the Father in the tomb and upon the cross.

So that we would know the truth, Jesus gave His life.

In John 8:32, Jesus spoke again of the power and importance of truth. *You shall know the truth and the truth shall set you free.*

How I pray you allow your soul to hear this eternal precept

for living:

No matter how powerful the lie may be, truth will remain unaltered. Truth is the first point of attack, so it must be our first line of defense.

Truth is fixed and appointed by God Himself. And because so, it will never matter how we feel, what our opinions are, what other's opinions are. Our circumstances, our losses, pains and troubles in this world will not matter. Truth will never move from its eternal position and it can never be altered. People can lie and even re-write what they believe or say is truth. But truth itself cannot be changed, it cannot be re-written.

Whatever happens, whoever rules, however loud anger, hatred and disdain raise its voice against truth, it remains unscathed, untouched and unmoved. It is the constant of God that man cannot contend with.

The search and drive for truth is unrelenting for the soul commissioned by God to lay hold of it. It's the lifelong quest for every one of us. Understanding the soul's deepest need, God placed over it an unchanging guardian of light;

TRUTH

He gave truth a voice apart from sound, a fire apart from flame and a faith apart from sight. Its presence abides with each and every generation. No matter how dark the times have been, it has never been overtaken or removed; nor will it ever be.

The prophet Jeremiah writes for God saying: *Roam to and fro through the streets of Jerusalem and look now and take note. And seek in her open squares, if you can find a man, if there is one who does justice and seeks truth...O LORD, do not Your eyes look for truth?* (Jeremiah 5:1,3)

King David, in speaking of God, tells us this in Psalm 51:6; *Behold, You desire truth in the innermost being, and in the hidden part You will make me know wisdom.*

The heart of God is to look deeply into the soul of His child and in the viewing find truth. This is His desire for us. Some of us search our whole lives trying to find purpose, meaning for living. We strive, ache and long to lay hold of something that we cannot name, describe or understand. We only know that if we don't find it, living is without significance and emptied of joy. It's the soul's internal drive to get to God.

Truth is the ordained avenue to Him. And because there is only one truth, then there is only one way.

One such truth seeker was a man by the name of Nicodemus. Nicodemus was from the upper class of society and a leader in the religious circle of his day. He was a Pharisee and a ruler of the Jews. A pretty lofty position to hold.

But Nicodemus had an inner struggle that was so persistent and consuming that it robbed him of sleep. Peace eluded him and when he could bare it no more, he turned to the only One he thought could give him the answers he was looking for.

Under the cover of darkness, Nicodemus seeks out Jesus, he seeks to know truth. Something, unexplainable to Nicodemus at the time, drew him to the Lord that night. His soul heard the unspoken call of the voice of truth and he found himself in the presence of Jesus. Read with me the account of this meeting with the Lord recorded for us in John 3:1-5.

Now there was a man of the Pharisees, named Nicodemus, a ruler of the Jews;

this man came to Jesus by night and said to Him, "Rabbi, we know that You have come from God as a teacher; for no one can do these signs that You do unless God is with him."

Jesus answered and said to him, "Truly, truly, I say to you, unless one is born again he cannot see the kingdom of God."

Nicodemus said to Him, "How can a man be born when he is old? He cannot enter a second time into his mother's womb and be born, can he?"

Jesus answered, "Truly, truly, I say to you, unless one is born of water and the Spirit he cannot enter into the kingdom of God."

Nicodemus knew the law of God; the Old Testament. He would have been trained and schooled in the writings of the Holy Scriptures. Of these things, he understood and had no problem with. Yet, there was one question he could not answer; one nagging thought that drove him that night. The need to know who Jesus was.

Like us, his soul was made to know Him, to love Him and bond with Him in living. What is the greatest question of all of life? What is the most important question addressed to the soul, the one that every soul will give an account for?

This ruler had a problem before him. He could quote the Torah in full, site the words of Jeremiah and no doubt Isaiah and the other prophets. But he could not explain Jesus. He had seen Him perform signs and wonders that no one had ever done before. He even goes as far to confess that surely God must be with Jesus.

Who is Jesus?

The struggle for Nicodemus was not believing that God was with Jesus, or even that He was sent from Heaven. His inner conflict was having to come to terms with truth and in so doing, acknowledge that his life would have to change. He would have to acknowledge his present reality of belief as a lie. Truth was before him.

Jesus' words were challenging to receive. He points Nicodemus back to his beginning place with God...the womb. *"Unless one is born again he cannot see the Kingdom of God."* Like anyone else hearing these words, he couldn't wrap his head around what Jesus was saying. He was thinking literally. His conclusion after giving thought to returning to his mother's womb as a grown man:

IMPOSSIBLE

Job, a man in the Bible who knew of suffering on a level that few ever will. He was a righteous man, fearing God and turning away from evil. Job pleased God so much that God bragged on him in Heaven before a great assembly. Even before the devil himself. A chain of events was set in motion that day. Job's entire family and possessions would be lost in a single day.

Messenger after messenger came in, one after the other, each reporting a tragedy to God's servant. What Job does in response to such news, is unheard of; a beautiful resolve to live. In the face of catastrophic loss, Job shaved his head, tore his clothes and fell to the ground and worshiped God. Upon that hallowed bed of tears, when there are simply no words to speak, Job worships His Creator; an abandoning of soul to the One who is far greater.

The first thing Job does is, he puts God in His proper place. This was Job's anchor of truth that he understood and lived by. His life would change, but God never would. He may lose everything dear to him, but he would never lose God. He yielded to God upon his ground of unspeakable sorrow. There, in the darkest hour of his life, he dropped an anchor of hope down into the sea of his grief.

Truth had not changed. It was still in place, unaffected and waiting on him in his greatest hour of need. It would hold him steady in the turbulence of hurt. When we are shaken to the core of the soul, we must fasten ourselves to the One who is unshakable.

Some of the most beautiful words in all of Scripture are found here in Job's moment of great crisis, as he laid his head before His Creator. His words hold immeasurable meaning for us. It is Job's soul cry and it is a hidden treasure of hope and wisdom for us today.

Then Job arose and tore his robe and shaved his head, and he fell to the ground and worshiped. He said: "Naked I came from my mother's womb, and naked I shall return there. The LORD gave, and the LORD has taken away. Blessed be the name of the LORD." Job 1:20, 21

In the very heart of Job's soul, he cries out, acknowledging where he came from but also to where he must return. He came from his mother's womb with nothing and with nothing he was going to return there. Job's soul resolved to go back to its beginning place; the womb of life. As it was with Nicodemus, we can only ask, how can this be?

What did Job mean by returning to his mother's womb? Job did not say he would return to the dust, meaning to die. On the contrary, he spoke of returning to the womb, meaning to live. It's an act that declares to all, *"my life is not over"*, *"this will not be the end of my life."*

I've often wondered what the messengers who delivered the tragic news to Job must have thought when they heard this. His words were spoken in worship. Job prostrated his soul in holy adoration before his Creator. His soul defaulted back to what it knew...God. The cradle of beginning where God was his sole source of life.

His soul went home.

Job knew that if he was going to make it, he had to allow God to start over. He believed that even though he had lost everything, even though his heart was crushed, his life was not over. With God, he could be reborn from the ashes of surrender. If you read the rest of Job's life story you come to see, without a shadow of a doubt:

Job was a soul reborn.

Hear his soul's cry that was heard on the other side of his losses. *God has redeemed my soul from going to the pit, and my life shall see the Light* (Job 33:28). God's humble servant had not only come out of the pit of his personal tragedies, but he now was full of hope for his future. He was looking ahead to greater good that was waiting on him. Job's soul had laid hold of truth.

This is the message Nicodemus needed to understand. His soul was crying out for truth. His soul was showing him the way home. We need to learn to listen to our soul. It has been taught of God. It knows it must find its way back to Him. Not just in the day of trial, like Job, but, in the day of salvation.

The challenge before the fragmented soul is this; there are many voices contending with this pilgrimage. Deceit waits to snare the hurting soul in the coils of doubt and chaos.

It's been said: *"In a time of universal deceit, telling the truth is a revolutionary act."* This was a revolutionary moment in the life of Nicodemus. He was confronted with truth and a pivotal decision was called for. His life would be forever changed. Eternity was hanging in the balance as he wrestled to understand, to know and find.

He wants to see Heaven; he has set his whole life up to this point of getting there. But how would he know the way? What assurance could be given him of his eternal destination? Jesus stood ready to show his soul the way home. He goes on to explain in John 3:6-11, 14,15:

> *"That which is born of the flesh is flesh, and that which is born of the Spirit is spirit. "Do not be amazed that I said to you, 'You must be born again.'*

*"The wind blows where it wishes, and you hear the
sound of it, but do not know where it comes from and where
it is going; so is everyone who is born of the Spirit."*

*Nicodemus said to Him, "How can these things be?"
Jesus answered and said to him, "Are you the teacher of
Israel and do not understand these things?*

*"Truly, truly, I say to you, we speak of
what we know and testify of what we have seen,
and you do not accept our testimony.*

*"As Moses lifted up the serpent in the wilderness,
even so must the Son of Man be lifted up; so that whoever
believes will in Him have eternal life."*

I love the words, *"truly, truly"*. Jesus is saying, truth, truth! This is
the truth Nicodemus. The Lord is referring to His death at Cal-
vary, when he speaks of Moses lifting up a snake on a pole. This
is an event that a Pharisee would have known, being a student of
the Old Testament. Numbers 21:5-9 details this account for us.

I have intentionally used the King James Version (KJV) because
it uses the word soul which is important for us to see.

*And the people spake against God, and against Moses,
"Wherefore have ye brought us up out of Egypt to die in the
wilderness? for there is no bread, neither is there any
water; and our soul loatheth this light bread."*

And the LORD sent fiery serpents among the people, and they bit the people; and much people of Israel died.

Therefore, the people came to Moses, and said, "We have sinned, for we have spoken against the LORD, and against thee; pray unto the LORD, that he take away the serpents from us." And Moses prayed for the people.

And the LORD said unto Moses, "Make thee a fiery serpent, and set it upon a pole: and it shall come to pass, that every one that is bitten, when he looketh upon it, shall live."

And Moses made a serpent of brass, and put it upon a pole, and it came to pass, that if a serpent had bitten any man, when he beheld the serpent of brass, he lived.

God's people had a longing of soul that could not be satisfied. They were miserable and thought it was because of the food they were eating. The want of temporary pleasures formed upon their tongue a hatred for life, for Moses, and God. They were in a bad place spiritually. Jesus wanted Nicodemus to understand what the real problem was.

Just as Moses lifted up a way to be saved from physical death, Jesus would be lifted up on a cross to save from an eternal death. Like in the day of Moses, the way to be saved from the sting of sin would be raised up on a wooden cross for the world to see. And all who look upon it for salvation, will be saved.

Jesus said, *"If I am lifted up from the earth, I will draw all men to myself."* (John 12:32) It wasn't enough for Nicodemus to believe Jesus was a teacher sent from Heaven, or a miracle worker who had God with Him; he needed to be born again…a spiritual birth from the womb of truth. The cradle of his own surrender. Yielding his will and his life at the feet of Jesus as his personal Savior.

The soul of Nicodemus was urgently trying to get to God, to that relationship he had with God in the womb of life. But he needed a way to get there. Nicodemus didn't know how to get back to God because he didn't know the way.

Jesus gives us the answer that Nicodemus was struggling with finding that night: He said, *You know the way where I am going. …I am the way, and the truth, and the life; no one comes to the Father but through Me.* (John 14:4,6)

Again, testifying of Jesus, the scriptures tell us this in Acts 4:12, *And there is salvation in no one else; for there is no other name under heaven that has been given among men by which we must be saved.*

The soul longs to return to God but there is only one way given in which to do that. It is the way that Job took and countless others, over the centuries of time.

Jesus

Jesus is the soul's way home. He is the soul's second birth. Apart from Him, the soul cannot be reborn in order to enter the Kingdom of Heaven. There has been no other answer given for the great need of the human soul, no other way, no other method or means offered. No other door of entrance or passage given.

Only Jesus.

Surely Nicodemus, upon hearing Jesus speak of His approaching death on the cross, must have been even more puzzled. He must be reborn, and for that to be possible, Jesus had to die. No doubt the question of how quickly faded into the shadows of why?

Why would such a One die for me?

The Love of God.

No matter which direction you look in God's Word, you cannot escape the everlasting and unfathomable love of God. Listen to the why given to Nicodemus by Jesus in this same conversation. (vs 16 & 17)

> *"For God so loved the world that He gave*
> *His only begotten Son, that whoever believes in Him*
> *shall not perish, but have eternal life*
>
> *For God did not send the Son into the world to judge the*
> *world, but that the world might be saved through Him."*

This was a soul to soul conversation. Jesus was speaking right the soul of Nicodemus. A soul to soul level of dialogue; a holy communion of grace, bending near on the plains of the dusty earth to reach and lay hold of a lost soul. A soul misplaced to tradition and religious standards of self-righteousness. A soul wandering aimlessly in the fields of performance and knowledge without wisdom. *Always learning, but never able to come to the knowledge of truth.* (2 Timothy 3:7)

God is love. (1 John 4:8) And Love was calling.

Our internal struggles, if left unchecked, and unchallenged, will become external deterrents for receiving Jesus. The saddest of all grievances is a soul that has yet to be reborn because it has believed a lie. Charles Dickens once said, *There is nothing so strong and so safe in an emergency of life as the simple truth.*

Truth clothes itself with the love of God and in the unrelenting pursuit of the soul, it sets out on a mission of grace. It wanders through the lowliest of places, the deepest pits of despair. It wades through the muck and the mire, calling, whispering, shouting and drawing us out into the light. It beckons us home. It echoes upon the pages every day of our life, exposing and calling out every lie, contending with deceptive allures, stripping down every wall, even our own theology and carnal pursuits.

Truth will not go quietly in the night. Not while there are souls dying in the darkness. It is the holy hound of Heaven. With every sunrise upon our days, truth calls to each and everyone one of us. Truth waits for the soul to reply.

Here is simplicity. Because God loves us so much, He refused to let us go on in life without a way to come back to Him. It's that all-consuming, overwhelming love of God for His child. Just as your soul has been desperately trying to find the way back to Him from birth, He has been pointing at and leading you to Jesus.

Jesus is the only way and the unfailing way.

Christian recording artist, LaCrae said, *The less time you spend with truth the easier it is to believe lies.* The battle for truth is so fierce because of what's at stake: the human soul.

Like Nicodemus, we all are searching for the truth. His soul understood that Jesus was the answer. There's something amazing that happens when the soul looks to Jesus. 2 Corinthians 3:16 tells us: *Whenever a person turns to the Lord, the veil is taken away.* The moment Nicodemus turned to Jesus for the answer to eternity, the understanding for who Jesus was, God lifted the veil from his eyes. God turned the lens of his spiritual sight to 20/20 power until Jesus came into perfect focus.

No matter what your soul has been taught, no matter where your soul finds itself today and no matter where your soul has been; it can always come back to God. It can always cry out to Jesus and *all who call upon the name of the Lord, shall be saved.* (Acts 2:21)

Lead me in Your truth and teach me, for You are the God of my salvation… (Psalm 25:5)

Who is Jesus to you? Have you been reborn?

A soul, once conscious of its power cannot be quelled.

———

AUTHOR UNKNOWN

CHAPTER SEVEN

A SOUL ON FIRE

I love to read, especially mysteries. I have since I was a little girl. Trying to work the storyline and figure out the *"who done it"*, appeals to my analytical mind. There's only one problem, I am not a patient person. In fact, I'm terrible at it. Waiting is torture. So, it's a great challenge for me not to give into the temptation to turn to the end of the book.

I want to see how it concludes, even before I have read how it begins. If I know how it ends, then the events that occur between the starting line to the finish line won't be so difficult to swallow. I can keep a reign on fear and speculation if I have the answer before the question even arises. Short cuts to being in the know appeal to this reader because it removes the need to trust in the waiting. Especially when it comes to living.

Sound familiar?

Life is our great mystery, it always has a surprise ending. It reads like a good novel, never knowing what's waiting for us in the next chapter. Page after page, the days roll on and events unfold before us; each having its own unique equations and demand for answers. Many unwanted and even unexpected, but never without purpose and meaning and the potential to change us and reveal who God is.

Try as we may, the chapters and events before us are hidden from our view. We cannot see what's next, let alone how it will end. It's been said that the future is veiled in mercy, meaning for our own good. This is why life is a glorious, yet, terrifying mystery. We can look back, only from where we are now and see a panoramic view of the yesterdays.

This viewing can become a well for us to draw from for many reasons. Sometimes to make the bitter sweet, while at other times to turn the sweet into bitter. The past cannot be re-written, it can only be remembered. Life doesn't come with an eraser.

Like other young girls in the early 80's, I had only one desire after graduating from high school and that was to get married. I know it sounds unambitious but to me, it was the greatest goal someone like me could have. I dreamed of my wedding dress, who I would pick for my bridesmaids, the food, the flowers and all the romantic details needed to make a perfect day. After all, I had dreamed of this day my whole life.

Steve and I married when I was only 18 years old. He had just finished a 4-year tour of duty in the Marines and I had just graduated from high school. We were barely saved. I've often said that when we got married, our clothes hadn't dried from the baptismal pool. We were not only young in life, we were babies in the Lord. Common sense isn't a wedding gift you need in order to set up house!

Two babies standing before the preacher, facing the unknown without a care in the world. My greatest concern in that moment was the huge pincher bug that flew in the door just as I began walking down the aisle. And would we make it to the airport in time to catch our flight after the reception. All important stuff when you are pledging your life away, right?

We said our vows and as we would come to find out, a story began. God began writing a new story. Two lives merged into one life. Two stories now intersecting upon the pages of life. It was a brand-new chapter. We were so naïve, and so immature that we never even thought about the ending. We never even wondered. And we never imagined that the story He began writing that day wasn't about "us".

Were we doing the right thing?

Is this what God wanted for us or only what we wanted?

Being in the will of God? What was that?

And our voyage began. I had to take some time to sit down with God and be brave enough to open up the book of our lives and start at ththe e beginning. For some, it may not be a difficult thing to do, but for me, it calls for courage and permission for my soul to cry over the ruins that I know are there in specific moments of time. Painful places where we found ourselves utterly crushed beneath the grief of our losses.

Looking back, from this vantage point, from this page of my life, I can see more clearly. My eyes can see two lost desperate souls in search of happiness. Grasping for fulfillment and wanting adventure. Running headfirst without a plan and apart from knowing the details, into a future we believed would deliver us from our current situations.

It's taken me years to comprehend the grievous reality we were facing at that matrimonial moment that drove us to say "I do" forever. We were using an unknown future to rescue us from our known present. We made each other our savior, our happiness, our reason for living. And we had no idea of what we had done. The sign on the back of our getaway car should have read, *"in trouble"*, rather than *"just married"*.

A story of love was being written, not between a man and a woman, but rather, between a soul and God. Two souls to be exact. I believe God was seated on the throne on August 7, 1982 in full sovereignty. And as His presence gathered around us that day He said, *If only you could see what I see.* Soul to soul, God began writing our love story and our journey home to Him.

We thought we knew what love was, but God would teach us,

show us, and engrave it upon the very tablet of our hearts. His love is the story. Line by line, page by page and chapter by chapter. At times, it has been obscured from our view by the tragedies, the mistakes, and losses of our lives; the clouds of despair blocking our view of the good waiting just beyond the storm.

God blessed us with two beautiful daughters; Stephanie and Kristen. To our family, He has also given seven grandchildren with the eighth on the way. I'm in the season now, the page of living, where if I stood to count the blessings of God from the beginning, I would find them innumerable to count. Many times, blessings come out of our greatest losses. This was to be so with me and Steve.

Our family was torn apart after 25 years of marriage. The loss and pain were unbearable. The hurt too deep for words and beyond remedy. I will not place blame here upon these pages. The details are written upon the pages of mine and Steve's story, reserved for God's eyes only. But God can take the bitter and make it sweet.

Upon this page of our story that I speak of now, it is still a boundless and stunning mystery. Our family was but ashes. So far removed from what it had been. As far as we could see, there was nothing good before us.

The years began to pass, during which time, God had been at work in each of us.

Once believing that my life was over, it was really just starting.

God was taking me back to the womb of beginning with Him. Although I did not know it at the time, He would be taking Steve there as well. Tears are God's river of change. He was doing something new.

God raised me up, slowly and with great care and intention. He began calling me to fulfill my purpose. From birthing a ministry known as Jabbok Ministries to becoming God's author for Women's Bible Studies, hosting a daily radio teaching program that reaches all 50 states and over 100 countries worldwide, and sending me across the globe to teach His women His Word in countless churches and women's events.

While running away from the hurt and unbearable sorrow of life, I found that God carved a track that led straight to Him and His calling for my life. When my soul finally surrendered, collapsing into all He is, life began to spring forth. He became my husband. He became the love of my life, my partner and companion. God became my everything. This is what He wants for each of us. but sometimes He has to take everything from us to do it.

After about nine years had passed, my phone rang. It was Steve. He had not been well, and his health seemed to be deteriorating quickly. The doctors had run all kinds of tests but still he grew worse. His speech was slurred, and his voice was struggling to hold it together. He said, *Pam, I am going to die. I must choose someone to be over my care and my affairs. I have chosen you, if you will accept it.* He went on to say, *I know I have done a lot of bad things, but I am so sorry, and I ask you to forgive me.*

Steve had been diagnosed with ALS, also known as Lou Gehrig's Disease. It's a Motor Neuron Disease that has no cure. It meant that Steve would die within 1 to 3 years. It's a very sad and painful way to die. We were all heartbroken over the news. He loved his family so much. It was a crushing blow to an already broken family.

Steve was a soul of great regrets, we both were. But he was a soul on the way back to his God, back to his Creator. This was the real beginning of our love story. Not the one at the altar. That's the one written by human hands. It's that love story we've been learning of through the pages of this book. The love between a soul and its God. When the soul of one chooses to love the soul of another as God has loved it, this is the true enduring love story.

We had been given the grand assignment to prepare Steve to go home. To be his earthly escort to his heavenly abode. There would be much to do, to assist him in this precious transition. Steve's race was almost over. The finish line had been drawn and was slipping into view. He would finish strong.

My soul struggled over this place. All of the hurt and loss I had buried beneath the busyness of ministry and life was now being unearthed. I knew that God wanted our family. He wanted all of us. I fell before the Lord and poured out the anguish of my soul.

Not in words, but in tears…my soul cried. It cried out to the Living God. I wept for Steve, for our daughters, grandchildren, and even for myself.

When there are no words, the soul can cry.

Sometimes it's okay to cry for yourself; for your sorrows. It may be difficult to understand this, but I was grieving over the grief of it all. My tears were for the thorn of sorrow itself that had pierced our hearts. Even now, I carry the sadness of it.

I rehearsed in my memory the heap of ruins that our family had been reduced to. How could we endure more loss? We had nothing but ashes that remained. It was a pile of sorrow, stacked high with regret and loss. This was all my soul could see. If I looked back, there was no hope. If I looked ahead, there was no hope.

So, I chose to look up.

Only as God can, in the might, yet tenderness of His being, He whispered to my soul; *"I'm the God of what's left."*

Even when we have nothing left, God can begin again. We can come completely empty-handed to Him and He can still do glorious things, above and beyond all we could dream or even hope. He's pretty good with leftovers! It was all we had to give Him.

Concerning the soul in need, the Psalmist wrote: *He will call upon Me, and I will answer him; I will be with him in trouble; I will rescue him and honor him. With a long life I will satisfy him and let him see My salvation.* (Psalm 91:15-16)

Sometimes God breaks us in a bunch of tiny pieces because He intends to feed the multitudes with the fragments of our life. This was true of me and Steve and our family. The pieces of our brokenness are still feeding souls today. Through sickness, God brought healing. In brokenness, He made us whole. Through death, God brought life and through great sorrow, He brought fulness of joy.

Steve lived a year and three months past his official diagnosis. He died at our home, surrounded by his family. We sang his soul to Heaven and sweet was the sound as God drew him up to be with Him. He made his way back home on New Year's Day. How fitting for God to design such a homegoing. It was bitter sweet. Only God.

Just when we are ready to close the book on our story, God begins a new chapter. One totally unexpected and apart from explanation. The tragedies of our lives are but seedlings of beauty waiting to come forth in our ordained springtimes. We never know what waits for us on the other side of obedience; beyond the gate of trust.

After his diagnosis, whenever he would catch us crying, Steve would say; *"Don't cry for me. I haven't received a death sentence, I've been given a LIFE sentence."*

He had it right. He would also say to me; *"Pam, now after I'm gone, you be sure and tell everyone about my life sentence".*

His sickness became a life sentence for all of us. This truth comforts us and dries our tears. It relieves us from the drive to understand why. God was too good in the midst of it all; too kind in the gifts He bestowed upon us, for us to tarry in the lowlands of why. The why's of living are found in the ashes of our graveyards of regret and in the valleys of the "if onlys".

Our past failures will try and call to us. When they call, because they will; don't answer. They have nothing new to say to us. Call your soul to look to the land of the living, to look up not around. For every loss, you will see God's greatest gifts hidden in the suffering of it. Caring for Steve was one of the greatest and most rewarding gifts of my life.

Your soul's love story is being written. The day you began on a quest to know Him, to see Him and serve Him with your life. For this we know; *He satisfies the longing soul and fills the hungry soul with goodness.* (Psalm 107:9)

No matter what you are facing, follow the script of His love. Untold beauty and grace are waiting. They are within your reach, no matter how scarred your hands may be.

> *Come & hear all you that fear the LORD and I will tell you what He has done for my soul.* Psalm 66:16

He is my love story.

Is He yours?

To fall in love with God is the greatest romance;
to seek Him, the greatest adventure; to
find Him, the greatest human achievement.

—

ST. AUGUSTINE

CHAPTER EIGHT

A LOVE WORTH STAYING FOR

Moved by the Living God, the prophet Isaiah wrote, ...*O LORD, we have waited for You eagerly; Your name, even Your memory, is the desire of our souls. At night my soul longs for You, Indeed, my spirit within me seeks You diligently...*" (Isaiah 26:8-9)

This faithful prophet knew God. Isaiah was God's servant and voice to the nation of Israel, yet his mission statement is clear and without apology; Isaiah longed for more of God. His life was a torrent of spiritual desire, longing for God to have all of Him and to allow him to have more of God. His chosen path of pursuit would cost him everything while laying up an eternal treasure the world could never steal.

Cover to cover and beginning to end, God's Word speaks of men and women who had reached a place in their lives where only one thing mattered; a narrowed focus upon only One. God. Nothing and no one else compared. They did not count the cost, only the price to pay if they missed Him, if they fell short of the finish line.

These are not people who did not know God, on the contrary,

they did know Him. Yet they ran after Him all the harder. A.W. Tozer wrote: *To have found God and still pursue Him is the soul's paradox of love.* It is the internal drive of the soul; a beacon that beckons, draws and presses onward until the last breath on earth is drawn. And when such souls have reached their end, not one has regretted the decision to want more of God… more of Jesus.

One such life, found in God's Word, holds great meaning and inspiration for my own life. She has influenced me beyond what words can pen upon these pages. Her name is Mary Magdalene. The name Magdalene means, "monument or tower". In other words, she represents something for us. She stands as a pillar of influence that we do well to look into, learn and understand.

Her life is one of overwhelming darkness that came into everlasting Light. She was a demoniac. Living inside of her were seven demons. Mary was completely taken over by the kingdom of darkness. When we read in Scripture other accounts of demoniacs, we realize quickly that their everyday lives were horrific.

Luke chapter eight gives these accounts for us as well as Mark and Matthew. In describing their lives, we're told they would cut themselves with stones, live among the tombs and cry out day and night. Whenever they were chained or tied down to restrain them, they would break their fetters and run away. The demon possessed would not wear clothes, and they would shout and attack anyone who tried to pass by the road where they were.

Their tortured state was one of disorder, pain and suffering. They lived as a wild animal no one could tame or capture. To have a mind and life lost to the control of Satan and his kingdom was a fate worse than death.

No doubt their lives were inexpressibly unbearable. What torment for a soul to be under the complete control of darkness and have no one who can set them free.

Mary Magdalene was that soul. Although we are not told of the details of her suffering in this state, we can know from the other accounts that it was a difficult life to have. One we can't begin to imagine. Then one day, Jesus came to her village, stepped into her life and everything changed. He called her out of darkness and set her on a new path of worship and service.

When we read about the life of Jesus, Mary is chronicled in some of the most important times of His earthly ministry. She followed Jesus in service, even contributing to the ministry. She was a faithful supporter. When Jesus was nailed to the cross, John 19 tells us that she was standing by the cross, as He suffered and died. When all but one of the twelve had deserted Jesus, Mary stood by Him.

After Jesus died, a man by the name of Joseph of Arimathea along with Nicodemus, our seeker by night, requested for His body. But who else is there, following the dead body all the way from the cross to the tomb? Mary Magdalene. She wanted to see where they laid Jesus' body. She never ran; she remained faithful to the very end and beyond.

Mary refused to leave her Savior. Her soul denied comfort and acceptance. She would not abandon her Lord, the One who saved her. This love compelled her even in the darkest hour of her faith. Jesus had died. How could they have killed Him, if He was the Son of God. How could He save her, if He couldn't save Himself? No doubt that others were wondering about these things.

Where were the disciples? Why were they not still following after Jesus? Had loyalty and commitment to the Lord died as well?

Did death eradicate who Jesus was?

Was the cross writing the Savior's ending?

Had death won?

Or worse yet, was it over?

Not to Mary it wasn't. I have no doubt the anthem of her soul was Psalm 63:8 which declares; *My soul follows hard after Thee.* I love the meaning found in the phrase, *"follows hard"*, that's used in this verse. The Psalmist is very intentional in his wording. This phrase means: *To cling, stay close, cleave, stick, join, stay with, pursue closely.*

Mary had this staying love. Her soul didn't stop loving Jesus at the cross, and it wasn't going to stop loving Him at the grave. In earthly reasoning, there was nothing Jesus could do for Mary now. No miracles to see, no sick to heal, or multitudes to feed, no storms to calm or dead to raise. Why would Mary stay, when Jesus could no longer provide these things?

In her eyes, Jesus was a love worth staying for. Even after He had been dead for three days, we see Mary coming early in the morning to the tomb. In this is love. A love that never lets up, refusing to quit, to leave or abandon, even in the face of death; even when all hope is lost.

When Mary and the other women who were with her came to the tomb that morning, something terrible had happened. (or so they thought). The stone was rolled away, and Jesus' body was not there.

Read what Mary does next upon seeing this sight recorded for us in John Chapter 20:

> *So, she ran and came to Simon Peter and to the other*
> *disciple whom Jesus loved, and said to them,*
> *"They have taken away the Lord out of the tomb, and we do*
> *not know where they have laid Him." ... John 20:2*

Not knowing what to do, Mary and runs to tell the apostles. She shares her news with Peter and John. They took off running to the tomb and low and behold they went inside and discovered that Mary was right. The stone had been rolled away and the body of Jesus was gone. When they are first told this news by

Mary and the other women, Scripture tells us that they thought it was nonsense.

They run to the empty tomb in unbelief. There was no faith in their journey. What's important for us to also know is this: When Mary and the other women first came to the tomb that morning, two men in dazzling apparel appeared to them and told them that Jesus was not there but that He had risen just as He had said.

Despite this encounter, Mary's message was clear to the apostles: *They've taken away His body and we don't know where they have laid Him.* Although Mary loved Jesus and she followed Jesus, there was a deeper mission before her. Mary was being called upon to pursue the resurrected Lord. Even though she knew it was Jesus who had saved her, faith was calling for her to believe in something she could not see, touch or feel; a faith beyond her initial encounter with Jesus.

To believe in the unseen was the great conflict of Mary's soul. There it stood facing her down upon the horizon of faith. The greatest pursuit and the costliest comes after salvation. Mary had come face to face with the question that Nicodemus was faced with:

Who do you believe Jesus really is?

Is Jesus who He says He is?

Is He more to you than just your deliverer?

Is Jesus your Lord beyond the grave, outside your line of sight?

Mary suddenly finds herself alone, fronting an empty tomb and coming face to face with her empty faith. When tested, the reality of her unbelief surfaced before her like a dark ominous cloud. But even in the confrontation of this moment, her soul refused to run away. I love her stance of permanence; *I will not be moved. I want you to take me to my Lord. Just give me Jesus…He's all I want.*

Read with me what happens next. Listen to the cry of Mary's soul as you take in the text of Scripture.

> *But Mary was standing outside the tomb weeping; and so, as she wept, she stooped and looked into the tomb; and she saw two angels in white sitting, one at the head and one at the feet, where the body of Jesus had been lying.*
>
> *And they said to her, "Woman, why are you weeping?" She said to them, "Because they have taken away my Lord, and I do not know where they have laid Him."*
>
> *When she had said this, she turned around and saw Jesus standing there, and did not know that it was Jesus.*
>
> *Jesus said to her, "Woman, why are you weeping? Whom are you seeking?"*
>
> *Supposing Him to be the gardener, she said to Him, "Sir, if you have carried Him away, tell me where you have laid Him, and I will take Him away."* (John 20:11-15)

What a woman! I've always admired her insistence that she would take care of the corpse herself, just tell her where He was.

It's that "I'll do it myself" mentality. No doubt, Mary was strong and passionate about getting to her Lord.

Jesus asked but two questions of Mary as she stood at the crypt of her Beloved. Every loss comes with the same challenge, the same questions that must be answered: Who are you seeking? Why are you really crying? What is at the core of your sorrow? Find the answer to this and you have the answer to life, even when you've buried the one you love the most.

When we cannot find the faith to believe what the Lord has promised or said He would do, the soul has the ability to track Him; to seek Jesus. The drive to get to Jesus remains in place, warring the good fight of hope that the grave combats to destroy. Our greatest challenges of faith will speak the loudest at the gravesides of those we love. Piercing through that bleakness, the voice of the Lord can still be heard.

The life of Mary gives us the only answer for these debilitating moments of despair; just give me Jesus! I may not have the faith, but Jesus I will still pursue. She was now left alone; isolated from the others who did not believe the pursuit at that moment was worthy.

Jesus wants to be our forever Way. Our forever Truth and Life. He stands ready to be our forever Lord and Savior; when the darkest and loneliest days of our life confront us, attacking the very core of our belief. If all we have in front of us is an empty tomb of despair, when we've lost our reason for living; Jesus can and will become our reason.

While Mary is pleading to find Jesus, she failed to recognize He was right in front of her. It's easy to lose sight of Him through the mourning of our grief. He was there, seeing every tear, hearing every pleading word of her broken and throbbing heart.

She was on the right track with Who she needed: Jesus. When her soul did not know what to do, it sought out Jesus.

Mary believed she needed to see Jesus, reach out and touch Him. What she was about to find out was this: she didn't need to see Him, she needed to hear Him. To know, *"What sayeth the Lord"*. Look with me and see what happens next:

> *Jesus said to her, "Mary!" She turned and said to Him in Hebrew, "Rabboni!" (which means, Teacher).*
>
> *Jesus said to her, "Stop clinging to Me, for I have not yet ascended to the Father; but go to My brethren and say to them, 'I ascend to My Father and your Father, and My God and your God.'"* John 20:16-17

Even at the graveside, Jesus had gone nowhere.

As soon as Mary heard Jesus call her by name, her soul awakened to His presence. She did not recognize Jesus by sight.

Why?

Because *faith comes by hearing and hearing by the word of God.* (Romans 10:17) Jesus called her soul to answer and recognize Him. Although she had served alongside of Him, watched Him perform miracles, stood by the cross during His crucifixion; she needed to know Him as her resurrected Lord. Mary needed to trust in Jesus by faith; apart from seeing.

No matter how much we have given, sacrificed or done for the work of the Lord, we must have a belief and surrender to the resurrected Jesus. It's that same call for the soul to go farther that it can see, hoping in what is not seen. This is where real life begins. There is no longer a need to see, to find, or even to be joined by another in our walk of faith. True faith can stand alone, even in the most critical hours of testing.

Doubt is exchanged for belief and loss is washed away through trust and renewed hope. Reason for living is discovered as we accept we were not made to live at the tomb of our losses.

The soul's love has staying power. Jesus is a love worth staying for.

> *The LORD is my portion, says my soul, Therefore I have hope in Him.* Lamentations 3:24

I'm on the hunt for who I've not yet become.

———

P J

CHAPTER NINE

THE GIFT OF SOUL

Seasons of life come bearing gifts, especially the older we get. Some gifts are not fully realized until another time, place and setting.

Many years ago, in the reign of Queen Victoria the Good, the Punjab came under the British Crown. The young Maharajah, then a mere boy, sent an offering to his new monarch. The wonderful Koh-i-noor diamond, and it was placed, together with the other crown jewels, in the Tower of London.

Several years later, the Maharajah, now a full -grown man, came to England and visited Buckingham Palace, asking to see the Queen. He was shown to the state apartments, and after making his obeisance to Her Majesty, he asked that he might see the Koh-i-noor diamond. Greatly wondering at his request, the Queen, with her wonted courtesy, gave orders that the jewel should be sent for, and that it should be brought under armed guard from the Tower to Buckingham Palace.

In due time it arrived and was carried to the state apartments, and handed to the Maharajah, while all present watched eagerly to see what he would do. Taking the priceless jewel with great reverence in his hand, he walked to the window where he examined it carefully.

Then, as the onlookers still wondered, he walked back with it clasped in his hand, and knelt at the feet of the Queen. "Madam," he said, greatly moved, "I gave you this jewel when I was but a child, too young to know what I was doing. I want to give it again, in the fullness of my strength, fully aware of what I give."

Streams in the Desert
Lettie Cowman

I love this story, for many reasons. The sheer beauty of it is captivating to me. Although the gift never changed, the cost to give it did. What was not painful to let go of in one season of life, may prove to be almost unbearable to part with in another. Perhaps it's because we come to see the value of the gift that had previously escaped us. And then again what was too costly to surrender on one day might be painless on another.

Hidden beneath the eyes of youth and inexperience can lie an immeasurable worth. It alludes our innocence and drapes itself beneath the cloak of our naivety. The young believer will lay everything down to follow God's plan, many times, not because their heart is completely His, but rather, they cannot comprehend yet what they've fully committed to.

Ignorance truly can be bliss in certain seasons of our lives. This paints a beautiful and accurate picture for us of our relationship with God. It's easier to lay your all upon the altar of sacrifice when you don't fully understand what that "all" is at the time of offering. But for the one who steps back in their tomorrow years that come, scanning the whole of their life, and in full view of what's at stake and says yes to God anyway; it's priceless in the eyes of Heaven.

I accepted Jesus Christ as my Lord and Savior just a few months before my 18th birthday. I was about to graduate from high school and because of my bad decisions, everything was spinning out of control. Wrong relationships, partying; you name it. My family had just gone back into church after being out of it for many years.

After warring with my mother over attending church with her, she finally put her foot down and made me go. I'll never forget her words, *If you're going to live in my house, you will go to church.* You'd have to know my mother, she never makes an idle threat. She meant business. At the time, I thought it was the most terrible thing she had ever made me do.

Turned out, it was the best thing she ever made me do! God was drawing me to Himself; calling me to Jesus. Through the guilt, shame and sin, I finally ran down the aisle one Sunday morning and surrendered my life to God. I did not fully understand salvation; not even close. But I understood and believed in who

Jesus was and asked Him to forgive me of my sins and save me.

Immediately, my lifestyle changed. There was no one who was more grateful for their salvation than I was. No convincing was necessary for me to believe I needed forgiveness or that I was a sinner. Fearful that people in the church would find out about the kind of life I had lived before, I thought that somehow, they would take back my salvation. As I said, I didn't fully understand what had happened.

At this place in my life, this page of God's story, I knew what it meant to give God my sins. All I had to give at that time was 17 years of living and 7 teenage years of rebellion. I could do that. It didn't seem that difficult to me in that moment. Sure, there were friendships, a boyfriend, and activities that had to be given up. It seemed like such a small price to pay considering the forgiveness given to me.

Surrender to Jesus as our Savior is not costly for us. Wanting to be saved for the soul that knows its lost, is natural. I've never heard anyone complain about receiving forgiveness. Everyone wants to be forgiven of the wrong they've done at some point in their life. Whether we will admit to that or not, but especially when we become a Christian.

Accepting Jesus as our Savior is the easy part. Accepting Jesus as our Lord…different story. Salvation is a two-step process. Read with me Romans 10:9-10:

...if you confess with your mouth Jesus as Lord,
and believe in your heart that God raised Him
from the dead, you will be saved;

for with the heart a person believes,
resulting in righteousness, and with the mouth he
confesses, resulting in salvation.

How I wish someone had explained that to me 38 years ago. We dive into Jesus heart first not fully knowing what is called for. A sinner who knows they're a sinner will snatch up forgiveness with no pressure or convincing necessary. Every soul has the inherited need to be saved. For this call to go unanswered, there has to be an all-out rejection; a defiance of what it knows deep within it needs to do.

When the soul steps up to this line of acknowledgment, two things are called for: belief and confession. Believing in Jesus' death and resurrection for the forgiveness of sins; this is asking Him to be our Savior. But that isn't enough. There must also be a surrendering to Him as Lord. Lord means, 'master, owner," one we serve and live to please.

Understanding this process, it is not hard to miss the price involved on both sides. Jesus gave His life to save us. We must give our life to follow Him. Yielding to Him as Savior and as Lord; this is when true salvation takes place. At 17, I believed in the price that Jesus paid, however, I was not convinced in the price I needed to pay.

There is a calling of every soul to deny themselves, take up their cross and follow Jesus. This involves a price; a costly one. Listen to Jesus' words as He explains this paramount truth for us.

> *Whoever does not carry his own cross and come*
> *after Me cannot be My disciple.*
>
> *For which one of you, when he wants to build*
> *a tower, does not first sit down and calculate the*
> *cost to see if he has enough to complete it?*
>
> *Otherwise, when he has laid a foundation and is not able to*
> *finish, all who observe it begin to ridicule him, saying, This man*
> *began to build and was not able to finish.* Luke 14:27-30

Just as building a tower is costly, and the fear of falling short of finishing it, so is being a disciple of Jesus Christ. Christianity is not only believing in Jesus to save, it is believing in Him to follow; no matter what price it demands. There are many who believe in Jesus as Savior but have not surrendered to or believed in Him as their Lord.

Your soul is driven to give itself fully to Jesus. He is the way home to God; the truth we established already in our reading journey together. If Jesus is the way, then we must follow Him; and that means bowing the knee before Him as Master. Your soul will find itself at home in this place of abandoned living. It was designed to seek it out and yield to it unconditionally.

The further the journey takes us with Jesus, the more it will demand of us to surrender. When I first became a Christian, I didn't have much to lay down at that point. Later it would call for my marriage, my children, my job, my family, my friendships, my ministry, my health, my grandchildren, my dreams and plans for the future and more.

Opening the pages of God's Word to the book of Genesis, we find that Abraham is a perfect example of this understanding for us. He was a commonplace man of flesh and blood, yet he catches the eye of Heaven. God chose him for an assignment so all-encompassing and grand, that only eternity would be able to hold the beauty of it. The reach of his ordinary life would truly be extraordinary.

God calls for Abraham to leave his father's house, and his home-land, and set out on a journey to a place He was going to show him. It was surely an act of faith as he set out for an unknown land. Read with me the interruption God made in his life and the promises He made (Genesis 12:1-3):

Now the LORD said to Abram, "Go forth from your country, and from your relatives and from your father's house, To the land which I will show you;

And I will make you a great nation, And I will bless you, and make your name great; And so, you shall be a blessing;

And I will bless those who bless you, And the one who curses you I will curse. And in you all the families of the earth will be blessed."

But what did this first act cost Abraham? His brother had died and his father as well, so leaving his father's house and his land was not as costly as it could have been. It was the excitement of a fresh start, a new land to discover. So only with the promise of a blessing to come, his journey began with God. A pilgrimage that is still pouring out blessings today.

See this vibrant truth with me: ***Abraham is following God as the blesser.*** He had surrendered himself to God's blessings; to His salvation. The price had not been so much for him to pay. At this venture, at this page, in his story, the blessing far outweighs the cost. The scale is tipped in his favor.

True to His word, God brings Abraham to the land He spoke of. Little by little, God shares His plan with Abraham. God was going to use his life to bless all the families of the earth by giving Abraham and his wife Sarah, a son. Everything God had promised to do was based on this son yet to be born. Everything. Without the son, there would be no nation, no future and no hope.

God did bless Abraham and Sarah with a son. They had not been able to have any children and they were well up in age. Long past child bearing years. Though it was a long and challenging journey to get there, Isaac was finally born. The conception and birth were a miracle of Heaven. Young Isaac begins growing up and their family unit seems complete.

Then God comes to Abraham and this is what He says:

*Now it came about after these things, that God tested Abraham,
and said to him, "Abraham!" And he said, "Here I am."*

*He said, "Take now your son, your only son, whom you love, Isaac,
and go to the land of Moriah, and offer him there as a burnt offering
on one of the mountains of which I will tell you."* Genesis 22:1-2

If Abraham had known of this price before he ever set out with
God, would he have gone? Complete surrender to Jesus will grow
more difficult the longer you follow where He leads. Before setting out, Abraham could have asked God for the details; the how
long, how far, the where and why. But he doesn't.

God's bidding was enough at that moment; enough for the first
step made in trust. Abraham believed that saying yes to God
was worthy of that initial leave of the familiar. He was absolutely
worth saying goodbye to all he knew.

But what about now?

The stakes were higher, more painful.

There was more to lose.

We don't need faith in a conquered land. More faith was required
since that beginning point where they had started. Abraham's
journey with God had taken a turn. When he set out with God
in full faith and obedience, surrendering his homeland seemed
small and worth it. But now, how could he ever pay such a
price? If you follow Abraham's life, you quickly find that it was a

series of altars. One sacrifice after another. The closer he got to the promises being fulfilled, the greater the sacrifice to be made.

It's the cost that Jesus spoke of. Saying yes to God is like being handed a blank piece of paper, signing your name to it and allowing Him to fill in the rest. Courage is not required so much when we start out with God; when we first become a Christian. But the farther we journey with Him, the braver we must become.

The soul's greatest gift to give is, *"yes"*. Just saying yes to God; without knowing the particulars, apart from understanding why or even the end result. In this great yielding comes the greatest cry of the soul: *"Here is my life Lord, fill in the details as you wish."*

Missionary to China, Betty Scott Stam was a woman who understood the cost of building the tower, the price for saying yes to God's plan. In her inward struggle to say yes to God's will for her life, she penned this prayer:

Lord, I give up my own plans and purposes, all my own desires, hopes and ambitions, and I accept Thy will for my life. I give up myself, my life, my all, utterly to Thee, to be Thine forever.

I hand over to Thy keeping all of my friendships all the people whom I love and are to take second place in my heart. Fill me now and seal me with Thy Spirit. Work out Thy whole will in my life at any cost, for me to live is Christ. Amen

A life of Surrender
Nancy DeMoss Walgemuth

You may not know the way in which God is leading you, or what He's going to do once you get there. The future may be obscured from your view; but you can trust Him. Your soul is at rest with Him; when it is in the center of His will there is perfect peace.

Have you surrendered to Jesus as Lord?

The apostle Paul wrote these words; it is my soul's life verse:

> *But I do not consider my life of any account as dear to myself,*
> *so that I may finish my course and the ministry*
> *which I received from the Lord Jesus, to testify solemnly of*
> *the gospel of the grace of God.* Acts 20:24

God designed the soul to bow the knee, to have a master, to follow, yield and serve. Not to people or things, but to Him and to His Son, Jesus Christ. Because of this ordained make-up, if the soul does not surrender to Heaven, it will surrender to something or someone.

Why?

Its drive is to be a captive…His captive.

Within each of us there is a drive to fall at the feet of Jesus and cry out, "Master, Savior". Until we surrender our soul to Him, we will seek another to be master over us. We will hunt the world over for something or someone to rule over us; to have all of us. Some bow before the god of money, sex, materialism, vanity, careers, power, relationships, greed, pagan gods, political ambitions, desires, corporate positions, false religions, etc.

The soul was made for Jesus. Listen to the apostle Paul's words to the church of Colossi regarding Jesus:

> *For by Him all things were created, both in the heavens*
> *and on earth, visible and invisible, whether thrones*
> *or dominions or rulers or authorities--all things have been*
> *created through Him and for Him.* Colossians 1:16

We were made for Him. Not ourselves, not another…only for Him. And until your soul yields to this design, it will go on as a slave to that which will be lost in the end. You will be a captive. But of who…of what?

Who is master of your soul?

The soul's fulfillment is not in the saving, it is in the following, the surrender. This is the greatest gift of the soul…the ability to confess Jesus as Lord. You never lose by giving it all to Jesus. Could today you say to Jesus once again, at this place in your life:

"On bended knee, Lord, I give you my life once again, fully aware of what I give."

No one can tell you how to feed your soul like your soul…
listen to it.

———

CURTIS TYRONEE JONES

CHAPTER TEN

THE CRY FOR SIGNIFICANCE

The hunt is afoot…the charge has been given. Echoes from Heaven pour forth night and day, unceasing in their eternal call. The eyes of the Almighty ever scanning, hovering over the surface of the earth; treading the low lands, valleys and hidden places. He searches in the day and in the night. He is relentless, refusing to abandon His quest to lay hold of that one soul…that soul found in waiting.

Waiting for Him; loving Him and anticipating the desire of His heart. His prize is the soul that only wants Him; to belong fully and unconditionally to Him. And when He discovers such a rare and beautiful treasure, something miraculous happens.

For the eyes of the LORD move to and fro throughout the earth that He may strongly support those whose heart is completely His… 2 Chronicles 16:9

Completely His…What does it mean to be *"completely His?"* The word that is used here means whole, in full measure, perfect and finished. In other words; someone who is fully God's, perfectly and wholly His. This is the soul that He seeks to find, the love that He hunts for. And when He finds such a one, He moves in to give the strength of His support in full measure.

God is looking to take that soul captive, and in the taking, set out for eternity together. No longer two, but one; a holy communion forged that time and the sorrows of the world cannot break.

The more we give ourselves to God, the more He will give of Himself to us. When we resolve to let go of every plan and dream we have that we may find and do God's, He blesses us with all the power and support we need to accomplish it. He yearns to give Himself completely to His child; but His child must be completely His first.

We live in ambitious times. There's a striving to have more stuff, bigger homes decorated with the latest trend, a nicer car, manicured lawn, outdoor toys and vacation homes. The drive to succeed financially and earn a certain social status, to get that coveted position; working up that corporate ladder, these are all the norm. Those just starting out want immediately what it took their parents years to have.

Ambition.

Have, have, have, and then have more. It's that hidden drive to find contentment, fulfillment and purpose for living and working. Living for the weekend to enjoy the material things that we've accumulated becomes the goal. The source of true joy is replaced with the happiness of temporary pleasures.

We're bombarded with TV shows and social media venues that cultivate this drive. Contentment is lost when something nicer, grander and more extravagant is dangled in front of us. Suddenly, a home we were happy with is now outdated and needs to be completely re-done. Our backyards are not up to snuff and our wardrobes are sorely lacking. Everything is wrong, and unhappiness takes over.

So, we set out to fill our desire to have what everyone else has and what society has taught that we should have. We work, accumulate debt, and we work more only to dig ourselves in deeper to lenders. Before long, the demand to take care of all the "stuff", and the bill to pay for it overtakes us. The ambition to have now becomes the ambition to keep.

What are we to do?

How is the cycle broken?

How do we contend with the call to have more?

There comes a time when we have to take a good hard look at what's in front of us; what it is that we are pursuing in life. What is the goal of our life every day of the week and on the weekend? Where have I placed the sign that reads, *"My happiness is found here."* What title have I given fulfillment?

This is the battle.

As long as we are chasing temporary happiness, the chasing will never end. Why? Because we will never be able to lay hold of it. Material things and possessions will never make us happy in the end. True joy is found inward, so it cannot come from something outward; meaning the things we can work for and buy. Change the pursuit and you'll alter the end result.

Hear the words once again of the apostle Paul. He's writing to God's people; the church at Corinth. Hear his own testimony and the testimony of the other disciples who were serving alongside of him.

> *Therefore, we also have as our ambition,*
> *whether at home or absent, to be pleasing to Him. ...*
>
> *and He died for all, so that they who live might no*
> *longer live for themselves, but for Him who died and rose*
> *again on their behalf.* 2 Corinthians 5:9,15

This great apostle did not seek for a home, for money, property or any other thing but one…Paul's one desire was to be pleasing to God, to be found wanting only His approval. Even when he was not in their presence, he wanted them to know he longed to be the man God wanted him to be. God's people needed to understand that with salvation comes the power necessary to live selflessly; the hunger and drive to live for Jesus.

Listen to the one desire of the Psalmist's heart penned for us in Psalm 73:25-26.

Whom have I in heaven but You? And besides You,
I desire nothing on earth.

My flesh and my heart may fail, But God is the strength
of my heart and my portion forever.

How convicting are the words, "*and besides You, I desire nothing on earth.*" There was only one thing he wanted; only one narrowed desire in his life: God. *"I want You and only You God",* was the heartbeat of his soul.

Nothing compared to having God…nothing.

God was the ambition of his soul; to have more of Him than he did the day before. This confession doesn't come apart from denying self and turning away from all that would draw the heart away. It means identifying the contenders and removing them from view and influence.

When God made us, He hewed out a cavern of need and want that only He can fill. This was intentional. Nothing else and no one else can fill it, no substitutes were made. It is reserved for His presence…for His filling and for His good pleasure.

Listen to the exhortation Paul gives to us in Philippians 3:7-9,12. Take note of what he did to make sure he laid hold of Jesus.

But whatever things were gain to me, those things
I have counted as loss for the sake of Christ.

More than that, I count all things to be loss in view of the
surpassing value of knowing Christ Jesus my Lord, for whom
I have suffered the loss of all things, and count them but
rubbish so that I may gain Christ,

and may be found in Him, not having a righteousness
of my own derived from the Law, but that which
is through faith in Christ, the righteousness which comes
from God on the basis of faith, ...

Not that I have already obtained it or have already become
perfect, but I press on so that I may lay hold of that for which
also I was laid hold of by Christ Jesus.

What was the great apostle's spiritual secret? He counted all things loss when he compared them to the surpassing value of knowing Jesus. Simply put; there was no comparison between material things and having Jesus. He laid them side by side and made his decision, and never looked back. His soul resolved to let go of everything, holding nothing back and holding on to nothing else but the Lord.

This was his ambition. With every written word of Paul, this determination is seen and known; it is an undeniable thread woven throughout his ministry and life. There was no question who Paul was following hard after.

He cared for only one thing…just give me Jesus. His anthem resounds familiar with that of Mary Magdalene.

Charles Cowman, missionary to Japan and founder of Oriental Missionary Society said of his generation; *The world has yet to see what God can do through one soul that is completely His.* I believe such souls are so rare and unfamiliar that sometimes we miss them completely. How can we detect such a one we've never seen in our life before?

These words rise upon our sight once again...*completely His.* Completely, nothing left for self or the world...nothing held back or placed in a reservoir for holding...completely. The Lord must become our object of affection, our passion, our one pursuit and longing of heart. With Him in view, the things of the world fade into the shadows want. Once dimmed from our view, God can take center stage.

Amy Carmichael was such a soul. A missionary to South India to orphaned children as well as a gifted author, her soul's desire is evident in her writings. She wrote, *I wish Thy way. And when in me myself should rise, and long for something otherwise, then Lord, take sword and spear and slay.*

Amy understood that you can give without loving, but you cannot love without giving. The measure of your love for God will determine how much of you He has. God wants no substitutes for you. He doesn't want your money, your home, your children, your job, your time, or talents. He wants you.

If He has you, all of you, then everything that your life touches will belong to Him as well.

Pleasing Him is what your soul was designed to do. It's the true source of joy and one that cannot be lost in the end. Every soul longs for significance. Whatever drives you in life will become the source of that significance. Until the soul relinquishes its will unto the will of God, it will go on searching for what it will never lay hold of in its present course.

True significance is found when the soul becomes ***completely His***.

When I stand before God at the end of my life,
I would hope I would have not a bit of talent left and
could say, I used everything you gave me.

———

ERMA BOMBECK

CHAPTER ELEVEN

ETERNITY IN VIEW

The family had been called in; it wouldn't be long now. Gathered around the bedside of our beloved father, we anticipated the sorrow yet to be released, not upon our dad, but upon us; as if it had been poured up in a pitcher of reality just waiting to wash over us. Our eyes had seen his fight for life; his yearning to stay longer with his family. We could see the toll the treatments had taken on his frail body.

To ask God to keep him would be selfish. What was waiting for him was far better; of this we had no doubt. It is this truth that eases the pain of saying goodbye. When a soul is standing on the edge of eternity, we are but spectators who have been given front row seats to one of the greatest honors life can afford. Angels gather, they draw near and stand ready for that last beat of heart; this releases the soul from its earthbound home, allowing it to enter eternity.

In this, we rejoiced with our father. But the tears in saying goodbye were real and without invitation. The angel of death was coming and there was no human intervention that could stop daddy's departure from this world. In Scripture, death is referred to as, *"the shadow of death"*. Job 10:22 speaks of death as such: *A land of darkness, as darkness itself; and of the shadow of death, without any order, and where the light is as darkness.*

It was in this all engulfing shadow of loss we found ourselves waiting. At times, death seems to engulf and cave in upon our faith. Even though we believe in Heaven, death is still difficult for the soul to bear.

For all who have faced it head on with a loved one before them, these words in the Book of Job ring true and familiar. We were never designed to know death, let alone accept it. From the beginning, death was never a thought to be known, only life and life abundant. But sin coming into the world, brought with it death, giving it a doorway into every life to be born. *It is appointed for men to die once, then comes judgment.* (Hebrews 9:27)

Never do we feel more vulnerable, losing all control, than when we are staring death in the face. Such was this time when dad was dying. It was 1995 and the Atlanta Braves had just won the title to send them to the World Series. We watched the final game together with him earlier that afternoon sitting on the side of his bed. For a brief moment, time seemed to stand still, drowning out the certainty before us.

Dad had suffered for so long. Cancer had taken its toll and though he fought the good fight against it, his body was giving out. He was too young, not even sixty years of age. We had only known him for a short while; just over three years. God was good to let us meet and know him before taking him home.

Our father was a man of great sorrow, guilt and regrets for the lifetime of memories he missed out on. But we harbored none of that against him. His brief presence with us was a rare and treasured gift bestowed upon our lives. Standing by his deathbed, we knew it was an invitation extended to us by our Heavenly Father; speaking into our hurting lives; *"see what I can do, if you only trust Me."*

It was clear that we had been summoned into our father's life for this hour. We were to help his soul return home…to return in peace from his earthly struggles and regrets. My sister, myself and our brother, chose to give our dad this gift. What a tremendous assignment to take the hand of another and hold it all the way home to eternity; communing about God to the very end.

Every soul is in transit to its final destination. Our window of influence is but a vapor in time, but the impact we make can stay with them forever. We leave our marks upon the souls we encounter. They take a little of us with them into life and beyond. What if we remembered this before speaking, acting, or reacting. This holds true in every relationship we have.

What if, you and I, braved the journey with them on earth; fighting for their destination?

Think with me for just a moment in light of this:

How much of a difference could we make if we parented the soul of our children rather than just the child?

What if we loved the soul of our mate rather than just our mate?

What if we were to love the soul of the addict rather than just the addict?

What if we loved the soul of our leaders for the soul they are and not just their leadership?

What would happen if we saw the soul of our offenders rather than just the offender?

What if we laid our differences aside, including our political and religious views, long enough to see each other through the lens of grace?

What if we chose to love the soul as God has loved ours?

How different would our world be if we saw everyone for what they are...a soul; a living eternal soul?

Every soul, yours and mine, has the volume to be a vessel of grace... a source of the unfailing mercy of God, able to pour out upon the traveling soul of another. To choose to co-labor with our Heavenly Father to help others get back to Him...there is no greater life to live than that. What if we paused long enough, merciful enough, to care where they are headed?

From the day we are born, to the day we die, our soul is in motion; it is moving toward eternity. From our first newborn cry to the last at death, our soul is but a stranger in time waiting for the final call. Everyone you will encounter today, or even tomorrow, is an eternal soul heading to eternity.

Jesus spoke of this brief passage of life in a parable to His disciples in Luke 12:15-21 (KJV). Take note of the message that Jesus was trying to convey.

> *And he said unto them, take heed, and beware of c ovetousness: for a man's life consisteth not in the abundance of the things which he possesseth.*

> *And he spake a parable unto them, saying, The ground of a certain rich man brought forth plentifully:*

> *And he thought within himself, saying, what shall I do, because I have no room where to bestow my fruits? And he said, this will I do: I will pull down my barns and build greater; and there will I bestow all my fruits and my goods.*

> *And I will say to my soul, Soul, thou hast much goods laid up for many years; take thine ease, eat, drink, and be merry.*

> *But God said unto him, thou fool, this night thy soul shall be required of thee: then whose shall those things be, which thou hast provided?*

> *So is he that layeth up treasure for himself and is not rich toward God.*

It will not matter how successful we have been or how many possessions we own in the day our soul is commissioned to leave this world. None of those things will matter.

Although our father owned very little, he died a rich man. The last four years or so of his life he set his attention on God. Long before he got sick, he was getting well through the healing and forgiveness he found in Jesus. He had made his peace with God. His soul was a soul at rest.

Hear the words inscribed for us in Psalm 48:14 (KJV): *For this, God is our God for ever and ever: He will be our guide even unto death.*

I did not know my father until I was a parent myself. There were no memories to draw from of past birthdays or Christmas mornings. Until that first meeting, I had never seen him or spoke with him. He had never given my sister or I anything. But in the end, he gave us the greatest gift of all: peace in the face of death. He taught us how to love a soul to Heaven.

He removed the fear of death from us. His passing, though ever so grievous, was the sweetest time with God we had ever known. Heaven was real, and death was just the door allowing us to enter. And as he took his final breath, we knew that he was there…he was with the Lord. In an exhale, his fight was over and eternity began.

A precious lady in our church was dying, in her last hours of leaving this world. She was still very alert and as fearless as ever. With her friends and husband by her bedside she said, *Can you believe I'm about to go to Heaven with my hair dirty.* Patsy had not lost her sense of humor. Heaven was as real to her as that hospital room. Faith held her heart firmly in place agreeing with the words of the Psalmist:

For the redemption of their soul is precious, and it ceaseth for ever: That he should still live forever, and not see corruption. ...

But God will redeem my soul from the power of the grave: for he shall receive me. (Psalm 49:8-9, 15)

The mother of my friend Melissa, passed away just a few days ago. She knew she was dying and she had lived a full life. Ms. Mildred was a grand soul to know and love, a true southern lady.

About a week before she passed she told my friend, Melissa, *"I've been thinking and I'm worried."* Melissa asked her, *"about what?"* Her mother went on to explain; *"I've been thinking. What am I going to say when I see Dustin and Shane?"* (Melissa's sons) *"I'm afraid I won't know what to say to them?"*

Again, Heaven was real to her. You would have to know Ms. Mildred to fully appreciate the conversation. She was a woman prepared, always. And entering Heaven would be no different. Visualizing that reunion, she was rehearsing a script in her heart; as eternity began drawing near.

We can learn a great deal from Ms. Mildred's homegoing. Preparing for Heaven is necessary and comforting. It's a real place, being prepared for us. And if Heaven is preparing for us, shouldn't we be preparing for Heaven?

Jesus said, *"In my Father's House are many dwelling places, if it were not so, I would have told you. I go to prepare a place for you."* (John 14:2)

Jesus was speaking hope right into the very soul of His disciples. The soul was made for the eternal, so it has the capability to receive and believe this understanding. Heaven is its home, Heaven is real and being prepared for me.

Hear the words written to God's people at Corinth:

Therefore, being always of good courage, and knowing that while we are at home in the body we are absent from the Lord—for we walk by faith, not by sight—

we are of good courage, I say, and prefer rather to be absent from the body and to be at home with the Lord. (2 Corinthians 5:6-8)

The body groans in the physical sufferings that often accompany death. For the Christian, the true groaning is for the soul seeking its release to go to Heaven. Awaiting its arrival are the saints and our loved ones who have gone before us, the angelic host, the Lord and God the Father. It's a homecoming not known to mortal man. For this, the soul knows it was born…to be at home with the Lord forevermore.

Knowing this truth, this event, which is coming to all of us; what sort of men and women should we be? What should be our focus? Our drive? How should we treat our soul?

The great commission of Heaven for every generation, for you and for me is found in the words of the Prophet Jeremiah: *Thus says the LORD, "Stand by the ways and see and ask for the ancient paths, Where the good way is, and walk in it; And you will find rest for your souls..."* (Jeremiah 6:16)

The ancient paths are all but grown over today in the eyes of this generation. The destruction caused by the rain of rebellion and deceit has taken its toll. Overgrowth of ever emerging opinions and false discoveries cover its passage.

The voice of truth is calling, the good way is heralding its presence; it beckons from the portals of Beulah Land saying...this is the way walk in it. Stay to the ancient paths laid out for you before the foundation of the world. They are sure, safe and will never lead you wrong. You can stay the course, upon its way, through even the most difficult and challenging of passages.

Your soul is eternal. It's but a sojourner upon the earth. Every day of your life, you've been headed to eternity. When the body dies, the soul will live on.

Are your prepared for eternity?

Is your soul ready to return to its Maker?

When you take your last breath, will He be yours?

And when the final beat is heard pulsating from the chambers of your heart, where will the next beat of your soul find you?

Will it be found in Heaven?

If you are not sure, then turn to Jesus today…believing in Him and on Him. Lay it all at His feet and pick up His forgiveness.

If you know where you are headed, are you ready? Will you be found faithful, having done everything to please Him?

And for you…Heaven bound soul I say:

Run the race set before you. Fight the good fight of faith. Press on to know the Lord and refuse to let up until you have laid hold of the One who first laid hold of you. Never surrender, settle or question. Lay down every encumbrance that hinders, detours, or disrupts. Strip away all that glitters, distracts or disarms your pursuit.

Dig your heels in deep upon the good and faithful pathway of righteousness and placing your hand to His plow of service, follow hard until the sun sets upon your life and just as eternity begins to slip into view hear the voice of the Faithful One giving way to your soul saying…

Return unto thy rest, O my soul; for the LORD hath dealt bountifully with thee. Psalm 116:7 (KJV)

Cry out to Him today…even now…fall upon your knees and kneel before your Creator. Raise up a cry, casting off every restraint and release your soul cry to Him saying:

It's You O God…It is You that my soul wants.

He is the God of all your days…He is your soul's cry.

And when the lies of who you are assails your faith, speak this eternal truth to your soul. *"God loves me, He is for me, and my soul is in His hands. I am on my way home to Him. I am His soul's cry and He is mine."*